Range-Wide Assessment of Livestock Grazing Across the Sagebrush Biome

By Kari E. Veblen[1,2], David A. Pyke[2], Cameron L. Aldridge[3], Michael L. Casazza[5], Timothy J. Assal[4], and Melissa A. Farinha[5]

---

[1]Wildland Resources Department, Utah State University.
[2]U.S. Geological Survey Forest and Rangeland Ecosystem Science Center.
[3]NREL, Department of Ecosystem Science and Sustainability, Colorado State University, in cooperation with U.S. Geological Survey Fort Collins Science Center.
[4]U.S. Geological Survey Fort Collins Science Center.
[5]U.S. Geological Survey, Western Ecological Research Center.

Open-File Report 2011–1263

U.S. Department of the Interior
U.S. Geological Survey

U.S. Department of the Interior
KEN SALAZAR, Secretary

U.S. Geological Survey
Marcia K. McNutt, Director

U.S. Geological Survey, Reston, Virginia: 2011

For more information on the USGS—the Federal source for science about the Earth, its natural and living resources, natural hazards, and the environment, visit http://www.usgs.gov or call 1–888–ASK–USGS.

For an overview of USGS information products, including maps, imagery, and publications, visit http://www.usgs.gov/pubprod

To order this and other USGS information products, visit http://store.usgs.gov

Suggested citation:
Veblen, K.E., Pyke, D.A., Aldridge, C.L., Casazza, M.L., Assal, T.J., and Farinha, M.A., 2011, Range-wide assessment of livestock grazing across the sagebrush biome: U.S. Geological Survey Open-File Report 2011-1263, 72 p.

Contents

Figures

Tables

Conversion Factors

Multiply	By	To obtain
meter (m)	3.281	foot (ft)
square kilometer (km^2)	0.3861	square mile (mi^2)
kilometer (km)	0.6214	mile (mi)

Range-Wide Assessment of Livestock Grazing Across the Sagebrush Biome

By Kari E. Veblen[1,2], David A. Pyke[2], Cameron L. Aldridge[3], Michael L. Casazza[5], Timothy J. Assal[4], and Melissa A. Farinha[5]

Executive Summary

Domestic livestock grazing occurs in virtually all sagebrush habitats and is a prominent disturbance factor. By affecting habitat condition and trend, grazing influences the resources required by, and thus, the distribution and abundance of sagebrush-obligate wildlife species (for example, sage-grouse *Centrocercus* spp.). Yet, the risks that livestock grazing may pose to these species and their habitats are not always clear. Although livestock grazing intensity and associated habitat condition may be known in many places at the local level, we have not yet been able to answer questions about use, condition, and trend at the landscape scale or at the range-wide scale for wildlife species. A great deal of information about grazing use, management regimes, and ecological condition exists at the local level (for individual livestock management units) under the oversight of organizations such as the Bureau of Land Management (BLM). However, the extent, quality, and types of existing data are unknown, which hinders the compilation, mapping, or analysis of these data. Once compiled, these data may be helpful for drawing conclusions about rangeland status, and we may be able to identify relationships between those data and wildlife habitat at the landscape scale.

The overall objective of our study was to perform a range-wide assessment of livestock grazing effects (and the relevant supporting data) in sagebrush ecosystems managed by the BLM. Our assessments and analyses focused primarily on local-level management and data collected at the scale of BLM grazing allotments (that is, individual livestock management units). Specific objectives included the following:

1. Identify and refine existing range-wide datasets to be used for analyses of livestock grazing effects on sagebrush ecosystems.

2. Assess the extent, quality, and types of livestock grazing-related natural resource data collected by BLM range-wide (i.e., across allotments, districts and regions).

---

[1]Wildland Resources Department, Utah State University.
[2]U.S. Geological Survey Forest and Rangeland Ecosystem Science Center.
[3]NREL, Department of Ecosystem Science and Sustainability, Colorado State University, in cooperation with U.S. Geological Survey Fort Collins Science Center.
[4]U.S. Geological Survey Fort Collins Science Center.
[5]U.S. Geological Survey, Western Ecological Research Center.

3. Compile and synthesize recommendations from federal and university rangeland science experts about how BLM might prioritize collection of different types of livestock grazing-related natural resource data.

4. Investigate whether range-wide datasets (Objective 1) could be used in conjunction with remotely sensed imagery to identify across broad scales (a) allotments potentially not meeting BLM Land Health Standards (LHS) and (b) allotments in which unmet standards might be attributable to livestock grazing.

Objective 1: We identified four datasets that potentially could be used for analyses of livestock grazing effects on sagebrush ecosystems. First, we obtained the most current spatial data (typically up to 2007, 2008, or 2009) for all BLM allotments and compiled data into a coarse, topologically enforced dataset that delineated grazing allotment boundaries. Second, we obtained LHS evaluation data (as of 2007) for all allotments across all districts and regions; these data included date of most recent evaluation, BLM determinations of whether region-specific standards were met, and whether BLM deemed livestock to have contributed to any unmet standards. Third, we examined grazing records of three types: Actual Use (permittee-reported), Billed Use (BLM-reported), and Permitted Use (legally authorized). Finally, we explored the possibility of using existing Natural Resources Conservation Service (NRCS) Ecological Site Description (ESD) data to make up-to-date estimates of production and forage availability on BLM allotments.

Objective 2: We investigated the availability of BLM livestock grazing-related monitoring data and the status of LHS across 310 randomly selected allotments in 13 BLM field offices. We found that, relative to other data types, the most commonly available monitoring data were Actual Use numbers (permittee-reported livestock numbers and season-of-use), followed by Photo Point, forage Utilization, and finally, Vegetation Trend measurement data. Data availability and frequency of data collection varied across allotments and field offices. Analysis of the BLM's LHS data indicated 67 percent of allotments analyzed were meeting standards. For those not meeting standards, livestock were considered the causal factor in 45 percent of cases (about 15 percent of all allotments).

Objective 3: We sought input from 42 university and federal rangeland science experts about how best to prioritize rangeland monitoring activities associated with ascertaining livestock impacts on vegetation resources. When we presented a hypothetical scenario to these scientists and asked them to prioritize monitoring activities, the most common response was to measure ground and vegetation cover, a variable that in many cases (10 of 13 field offices sampled) BLM had already identified as a monitoring priority. Experts identified several other traditional (for example, photo points) and emerging approaches (for example, high-resolution aerial photography) to monitoring.

Objective 4: We used spatial allotment data (described in Objective 1) and remotely sensed vegetation data (sagebrush cover, herbaceous vegetation cover, litter and bare soil) to assess differences in allotment LHS status ("Not met" vs. "Met"; if "Not met" – livestock-caused vs. not). We then developed logistic regression models, using vegetation variables to predict LHS status of BLM allotments in sagebrush steppe habitats in Wyoming and portions of Montana and Colorado.

In general, we found that more consistent data collection at the local level might improve suitability of data for broad-scale analyses of livestock impacts. As is, data collection methodologies varied across field offices and States, and we did not find any local-level monitoring data (Actual Use, Utilization, Vegetation Trend) that had been collected consistently enough over time or space for range-wide analyses. Moreover, continued and improved emphasis on monitoring also may aid local management decisions, particularly with respect to effects of livestock grazing. Rangeland science experts identified ground cover as a high monitoring priority for assessing range condition and emphasized the importance of tracking livestock numbers and grazing dates. Ultimately, the most effective monitoring program may entail both increased data collection effort and the integration of alternative monitoring approaches (for example, remote sensing or monitoring teams). In the course of our study, we identified three additional datasets that could potentially be used for range-wide analyses: spatial allotment boundary data for all BLM allotments range-wide, LHS evaluations of BLM allotments, and livestock use data (livestock numbers and grazing dates). It may be possible to use these spatial datasets to help prioritize monitoring activities over the extensive land areas managed by BLM. We present an example of how we used spatial allotment boundary data and LHS data to test whether remotely sensed vegetation characteristics could be used to predict which allotments met or did not meet LHS. This approach may be further improved by the results of current efforts by BLM to test whether more intensive (higher resolution) LHS assessments more accurately describe land health status. Standardized data collection in more ecologically meaningful land units may improve our ability to use local-level data for broad-scale analyses.

Introduction

Domestic livestock grazing occurs in virtually all sagebrush habitats and is a prominent disturbance factor. By affecting habitat condition and vegetation trend, grazing may influence the resources required by, and thus, the distribution and abundance of sagebrush-obligate wildlife species. For example, livestock grazing is identified as a population risk to sage-grouse (*Centrocercus* spp.) in numerous local conservation plans (for example, Bi-State Local Planning Group, 2004; Northern Eagle/Southern Routt Work Group, 2004). Yet, the risks that livestock grazing may pose to these species and their habitats are not always clear, particularly at the landscape scale (Connelly and others, 2004; Crawford and others, 2004). An assessment of how livestock grazing management influences vegetation condition on rangelands is integral to our understanding of the long-term persistence of sagebrush-obligate wildlife species (Aldridge and others 2008).

Although livestock grazing intensity and associated habitat condition may be known in many places at the local level (for example, individual livestock management units), we have not yet been able to answer questions about use, condition, and trend of habitat, at the landscape or range-wide scale for wildlife in sagebrush ecosystems (Crawford and others, 2004). Increasingly, our ability to successfully manage these ecosystems will call for examination of conditions and patterns at broad scales (Chambers and Wisdom, 2009). A great deal of local information about grazing use, management regimes, and ecological condition exists for individual management units under the oversight of Bureau of Land Management (BLM), U.S. Forest Service, National Resource Conservation Service (NRCS), State management agencies, Tribal lands, and private landowners. However, the extent, quality and types of existing data across sagebrush habitat are unknown. This hinders the compilation, mapping, or analysis of these data to draw conclusions.

If quality data are compiled, we may be able to assess the status of existing rangelands across livestock management boundaries and evaluate habitat conditions for wildlife populations, and ultimately help identify priority areas for conservation and restoration.

The overall objective of our study was to perform a range-wide assessment of livestock grazing effects (and the relevant supporting data) in sagebrush ecosystems managed by the BLM. Specific objectives included the following:

1. Identify and refine existing range-wide datasets to be used for analyses of livestock grazing effects on sagebrush ecosystems.

2. Assess the extent, quality, and types of livestock grazing-related natural resource data collected by BLM range-wide (that is, across districts and regions).

3. Compile and synthesize recommendations from federal and university rangeland science experts about how BLM might prioritize collection of different types of livestock grazing-related natural resource data.

4. Investigate whether range-wide datasets (Objective 1) could be used in conjunction with remotely-sensed imagery to identify across broad scales (a) allotments potentially not meeting BLM Land Health Standards (LHS) and (b) allotments in which unmet standards were attributable to livestock grazing.

Section I: Identification and Refinement of Existing Datasets

We identified, often with assistance from Bureau of Land Management (BLM) personnel, four datasets that potentially could be used for analyses of livestock grazing effects on sagebrush ecosystems and that could be applied to a spatial land area: (1) Allotment data, (2) Land Health Standards (LHS) data, (3) Actual, Billed and Permitted Use, and (4) Soil map units with their associated Ecological Site Descriptions (ESDs) and forage production data. Below we describe the origin and potential uses of each dataset and summarize how we refined data for analysis.

Spatial Allotment Data

We obtained spatial allotment boundary data as a first step in our analyses. Because most monitoring and management occur at the allotment level, we anticipated that these data would form the basis of further spatial analyses. We first reviewed the BLM national grazing allotment spatial dataset available from the GeoCommunicator National Integrated Land System (NILS) website in 2007. We identified several limitations in those data and learned that some BLM States and/or field offices had updated their spatial data to rectify these limitations, but maintained the data outside of NILS. In some cases State Offices maintained an updated statewide dataset, although for other States the field office had the highest order of maintained data. We contacted appropriate BLM offices (State or field, 25 in all) to obtain the most recent data, assessed the data, established a development protocol, and compiled data into a coarse, topologically enforced dataset throughout the area of interest (that is, the pre-settlement distribution of Greater Sage-Grouse in the Western United States). Our goals were to develop a spatial product for mapping BLM allotments across the West, while limiting/eliminating problems associated with gaps, slivers, edge matching, duplicate polygons, and inconsistent attribution. The product could then be linked with additional tabular data, such as billed and permitted use and allotment-specific LHS and sagebrush cover data. A detailed description of the methodology can be found in appendix 1.

Land Health Standards (LHS)

We identified a dataset that contained results of LHS evaluations for all BLM allotments across the region as of 2007. The BLM performs periodic evaluations of region-specific LHS (appendix 2, table 2-1) to determine rangeland health. Standards were developed by BLM State Offices in conjunction with regional resource advisory councils, and evaluations of these standards are intended to be completed at the time of grazing permit issuance and renewal (every 10 years). In 2008, LHS data for all allotments in all regions were compiled by BLM in response to a Freedom of Information Act (FOIA) request made by a private organization. The BLM provided us with a copy of these data. The dataset provided three major types of information that were of interest to us: (1) date(s) (if any) of the most recent LHS evaluation for each allotment, (2) whether, when assessed, each region-specific standard (3–8, depending on region) had been met on a given allotment, and (3) whether livestock contributed to any of these standards not being met. A description of how we processed the original dataset to prepare data for analysis is detailed in appendix 2.

Actual, Billed, and Permitted Use

We examined actual, billed, and permitted use as potential metrics of grazing intensity on BLM allotments. Actual Use data are permittee-reported livestock numbers with turn-on and take-off dates for the livestock on the allotment. Completeness of this information relies on permittees completing those reports. Accuracy of the numbers and dates reported relies on both the honor system and oversight by BLM. As discussed in Section II, although Actual Use data were more available relative to other data types, overall the availability of Actual Use data across time and space was patchy and therefore generally lacking in sufficient coverage to be suitable for range-wide analyses.

Complete Permitted and Billed Use records, however, are maintained for all allotments administered by the BLM and are potentially more useful for range-wide analyses. Permitted use dates and livestock numbers are the legal maximum grazing amounts for a given allotment, and legal adjustments to these numbers occur infrequently (although this does not preclude annual negotiations between BLM and permittees for adjustments based on climate, forage availability, etc.). Billed Use information more closely reflects actual year-to-year grazing dates and livestock numbers. These billing records are maintained in the Rangeland Administration System (*http://www.blm.gov/ras/*) and are used for calculations of permittees' annual grazing bills. In Section II, we discuss relationships among these types of use records and their potential utility for characterizing livestock grazing effects.

Ecological Site Descriptions (ESDs) and Forage Production

Given the logistical difficulties of administering the vast land area covered by BLM, permitted stocking rates on some allotments may not necessarily reflect the most current production estimates or other supporting data (for example, water point locations or topography, both of which influence the amount of production effectively available to livestock). We therefore investigated the possibility of using spatial (GIS-Geographic Information Systems) NRCS soil map unit data and their associated ESD data to make current estimates of forage availability for livestock grazing on BLM allotments. These data could then potentially be combined with water locations and topography data (for example, Digital Elevation Models) to provide production estimates and identify allotments that might benefit from closer inspection and potential adjustment of permitted and/or Actual Use.

As a first step, we field-validated estimates of potential vegetation production gleaned from soils data (NRCS Soil Survey Geographic Database - SSURGO) and the NRCS Ecological Site Information System (ESIS). We made on-the-ground estimates of production, using the NRCS Reconstruction Method (U.S. Department of Agriculture, Natural Resources Conservation Service, 2009b), at 42 randomly located sites in Harney County, Oregon (fig. 1). Our samples covered nine different ecological sites in Major Land Resource Area (MLRA) 010 (Central Rocky and Blue Mountain Foothills; see appendix 3 for full explanation of site selection). We then compared those on-the-ground herbaceous production estimates to estimates for those sites contained in the ESIS database. Based on our sample, we found that our estimates generally fell within the production range outlined in the corresponding ESDs (fig. 2).

Section II: Monitoring of Livestock Grazing Effects and Expert Opinions

Summary

Public land management agencies, such as the Bureau of Land Management (BLM), are charged with managing land throughout the Western United States for multiple uses including livestock grazing and conservation of sensitive species and their habitats. Data on condition and trends of these rangelands—particularly with respect to livestock grazing—provide critical information for effective management of these multi-use landscapes. Accordingly, current grazing regulations require BLM to report rangeland condition on grazing allotments and use monitoring data to support stocking rate-related management decisions. Additionally, grazing permits are to be issued and renewed contingent on the meeting of State- or region-specific Land Health Standards (LHS). We therefore investigated the availability of BLM livestock grazing-related monitoring data in sagebrush steppe and the status of LHS across the Western United States. We then sought input from university and federal rangeland science experts about how best to prioritize rangeland monitoring activities. We found that the most commonly available monitoring data (≥ 1 year of data between 1997 and 2007) were permittee-reported livestock numbers and season-of-use (71 percent of allotments) followed by Photo Point (58 percent), forage Utilization (52 percent), and finally, Vegetation Trend measurement data (37 percent). As of 2007, 57 percent of allotments had completed LHS. Of those, BLM indicated 67 percent of allotments were meeting standards. For the 33 percent not meeting standards, livestock were considered the causal factor in 45 percent of cases (about 15 percent of all allotments). Our data inspections, as well as conversations with BLM personnel, indicated a need for greater emphasis on collection of grazing-related monitoring data, particularly ground cover. We highlight commonalities between BLM monitoring approaches and expert-suggested priorities, present ideas for making the most of existing historical data, and finally discuss emerging ideas for rangeland monitoring.

Introduction

Livestock grazing is a dominant land use on BLM lands across the Western United States. The Secretary of the Interior is charged in the Federal Land Policy and Management Act (FLPMA) of 1976 to "manage the public lands under principles of multiple use and sustained yield…" and "shall, by regulation or otherwise, take any action necessary to prevent unnecessary or undue degradation of the lands" (Public Law 94-579, Sec. 302). In addition to managing these public lands for livestock grazing, BLM manages for conservation of endangered and threatened species and their habitat. To do so, BLM aims to achieve appropriate grazing practices that will prevent land degradation and facilitate the sustainability and compatibility of grazing and conservation.

Rangeland Monitoring

Monitoring the ecological status of rangelands is integral to successful grazing management and for insuring that proposed improvements are effective (Williams and others, 2007). In an effort to improve unsatisfactory rangeland conditions and curtail any further degradation, the Public Rangelands Improvement Act of 1978 committed federal land management agencies to providing regular updates on the condition and trend of rangelands. Current grazing regulations also require that monitoring data and/or field observations be used to support any changes to allowable stocking rates on BLM allotments (43 CFR 4110.3).

Historically, monitoring of condition and trend on rangelands typically focused on plant community development (cover/biomass) in a successional framework, and vegetation recovery was assumed to occur following the lessening of grazing intensity (Dyksterhuis, 1949). However, in response to debate over the validity of the rangeland succession model (particularly the relationship between grazing intensity and vegetation recovery), Westoby and others (1989) proposed an alternative state-and-transition model. This model, in which thresholds govern management-driven transitions between different vegetation communities or states, has gained wide acceptance and recently been incorporated into the USDA Natural Resources Conservation Service (NRCS) Ecological Site Descriptions for rangelands (U.S. Department of Agriculture, Natural Resources Conservation Service, 2009a). A corollary of the state-and-transition framework is that monitoring of vegetation-grazing relationships should be expanded to include a greater complexity of ecological and physical processes or ecosystem attributes beyond vegetation (Herrick and others, 2005).

Despite progress in understanding what and how best to monitor, BLM monitoring efforts have been criticized over the last several decades as being hampered by funding/personnel issues and confusion and inconsistencies associated with monitoring approaches (West, 2003). It is not clear at regional, or range-wide scales which types of vegetation, soil, and livestock grazing-related monitoring data are being collected on BLM land, which methods are being used, or how consistently data are being collected, analyzed, and interpreted. Similarly, it is unclear whether these data are comprehensive and sufficiently consistent across time and space to make region-wide assessments of rangeland status or livestock grazing effects on rangeland status.

Land Health

Rangeland health indicators have long been used to determine rangeland status (West, 2003) and typically are used to evaluate specific rangeland attributes or LHS. Over time, this method has expanded from using just a few select indicators to including a broader array. In particular, there have been efforts to include indicators not only relating directly to vegetation but to other ecological processes such as nutrient cycling, soil stability and hydrology (Tongway, 1994; Pyke and others, 2002).

Changes in BLM rangeland policy have mirrored these changes in philosophy. In 1995, BLM identified fundamentals of rangeland health (43 CFR 4180.1; appendix 4) and created new grazing regulations that required each state, in consultation with relevant Resource Advisory Councils, to develop state or regional LHS and livestock management guidelines. These LHS and guidelines, subject to approval by the Secretary of the Interior, are required to address: (1) watershed function, (2) nutrient cycling and energy flow, (3) water quality, (4) habitat for endangered, threatened, proposed, candidate, and other special status species, and (5) habitat quality for native plant and animal populations and communities (43 CFR 4180.2). To assess whether standards are being met, BLM is required to perform on-the-ground evaluations of a suite of indicators associated with its State- or region-specific standards (appendix 2).

Since 1997, livestock grazing practices on BLM land have been linked to the status of LHS; if an allotment fails LHS due to livestock, appropriate corrective action must be taken and the terms and conditions of the grazing permit may be adjusted (43 CFR 4180.2). If an allotment fails one or more standards, ideally, monitoring data are used to identify causal factors (see fig. 3). If grazing practices are identified as significant factors resulting in failure, management actions must be proposed to help achieve compliance (fig. 3; 43 CFR 4180.2). This emphasis on identification of causal factors underscores the importance of access to supporting monitoring data. These land health standard evaluations also represent a potentially comprehensive, broad-scale dataset of land health status across western BLM land and may be useful for identifying relationships between rangeland health status and causal factors such as livestock grazing.

Objectives

The first major objective of our study was to address the availability and status of BLM rangeland health and livestock grazing-related monitoring data. Specifically, we (1) examined types, availability, and consistency of rangeland monitoring data from a sample of BLM offices that administer allotments in sagebrush steppe, (2) obtained and utilized existing BLM LHS data to ascertain rangeland health status across the Western United States, and (3) evaluated the degree to which data were available for identifying livestock grazing as a contributing factor in failure to meet LHS in sagebrush steppe. Our second major objective was to more closely examine current and potential future approaches to monitoring rangeland status and livestock grazing impacts on BLM land. In particular, we (1) compiled opinions of rangeland science experts about how best to prioritize rangeland monitoring activities, (2) compared and contrasted these opinions with current BLM practices, and (3) identified opportunities for new directions and making the most of existing BLM data.

Methods

Field Office Sampling

We visited BLM field offices to evaluate the availability of monitoring data commonly used for monitoring of rangeland status. These data types included: (1) *Actual use* – livestock numbers and grazing dates (self-reported by grazing allotment permittees), (2) *Utilization* – percentage of current year's vegetation production consumed by animals, and (3) *Vegetation Trend* – measures of community status over time, including both repeat photos and quantitative vegetation sampling. We also inspected files for presence of grazing plans or allotment management plans (AMPs), which can be written to help guide management of grazing allotments. These plans outline specific resource objectives relating to livestock grazing (for example, available AUMs, range improvements) and in the case of AMPs, also include objectives related to wildlife. Because plans must provide for monitoring to evaluate the effectiveness of management in achieving objectives (43 CFR 4120.2), we also investigated the presence of evaluations. We focused on data typically maintained by rangeland conservationists, and we did not inspect supporting data maintained by other specialists, including riparian (for example, PFC-Proper Functioning Condition), wildlife, or wild horse/burro data.

We inspected these data types for a total of 310 randomly selected allotments in 13 BLM offices (covering 15 BLM resource areas and 6 States) that fell within big sagebrush (*Artemisia tridentata*) steppe and potential Greater Sage-Grouse (*Centrocercus urophasianus*) range. In 1982, BLM began classifying allotments as "Maintain" or "Improve," with the intention of concentrating monitoring efforts on "Improve" allotments (BLM WO IM 82-292), so we stratified the 310 allotments to be one-third Maintain (n=109) and two-thirds Improve (n=201). We excluded custodial allotments from our sample because they typically are small, isolated pieces of federal land located within non-federal land areas. Our study focused on sagebrush steppe because it was included in a broader project focused on sage-grouse conservation.

Seven of the thirteen field offices we selected were among those already participating in a complementary BLM study aimed at exploring spatially explicit land health assessments. The remaining six offices were selected semi-randomly with preference given to offices with a history of cooperation or collaboration on previous or related projects. Thus, our BLM office selection may be biased towards those with a greater willingness to participate and share monitoring data.

For each of the 310 allotments, we recorded presence or absence of each data type (Actual Use, Utilization, Vegetation Trend, Photo Point, grazing/allotment management plans, and evaluations) for every year between 1997 and 2007. We did not include earlier dates because data prior to 1997 were more likely to have been archived and difficult to access. Data were counted as present if any data were present in the given year; inconsistent naming of sample sites and variable sample site locations over time precluded our ability to distinguish when data were incomplete within allotments (that is, data were counted as present even if they were only present for a subset of pastures or key areas within that allotment).

We also determined which of the 310 allotments had *not* met LHS (see below), and we examined which types of monitoring information had been collected to potentially support determinations that livestock were contributing to unmet standards. We also accessed BLM billing information for the 310 allotments contained in the Rangeland Administration System (RAS; http://www.blm.gov/ras/) and examined the relationship between AUMs of actual use (permittee-reported livestock numbers) and BLM billing records. Billed Use data are more comprehensive than Actual Use data (because they are maintained for each allotment each year), but it is not clear how closely billing records reflect actual use.

Land Health Standards Data

To determine LHS status range-wide, we used a dataset compiled by the national BLM office in 2008. Although specific standards varied across States in content and number (appendix table 2-1), we determined that several standards across all BLM regions fell into three broad categories relevant to livestock grazing: Upland, Riparian, and Biodiversity. The only exception was that the Mojave Region had no Riparian standards. Classifying standards into these three broad (and common) categories allowed us to examine patterns across the Western United States. We first identified allotments with LHS evaluations completed between 1997 and 2007. Then for each of those allotments, we determined if BLM rated Upland, Riparian, and Biodiversity standards as being met. If a standard was not met, we determined if BLM deemed that livestock contributed to failure to meet the standard.

Expert Opinions

We assembled, through informal conversations, opinions of 20 federal rangeland scientists (representing USDA-ARS in six States, NRCS in four States, and USFS in one State) and 22 university rangeland scientists (representing 13 universities) on how best to monitor rangeland condition and livestock effects within the logistical and time constraints faced by the BLM. We selected rangeland experts based on his/her membership in the Society for Range Management, professional reputation, and record of peer-reviewed publication in rangeland science literature. Conversations took place at the 2009 Society for Range Management annual meeting in Albuquerque, New Mexico, or over the telephone. We presented scientists with a hypothetical monitoring scenario asking them to prioritize activities for monitoring of livestock grazing effects on rangeland resources: "Assuming a new piece of land has been acquired by the BLM or some other land management agency, how would you set up a monitoring program to (1) monitor rangeland condition, and (2) determine livestock impacts (that is, make explicit connection between livestock grazing and land condition)? First, what would be the single most important field measurement, and how would you interpret that data with respect to (1) and (2)? Second, if you could instate a full monitoring program for that piece of land, what would you do? Assume that one person can spend ½ day per year collecting this monitoring information. Also, assume that the number of livestock, dates of livestock grazing, and climate/rainfall information will be collected (outside of your ½ day monitoring program) and made available to you."

Statistical Analyses

With our field office data, for each of the six data types (Actual use, Utilization, Trend, Photo Points, AMP/Grazing plan, and Allotment evaluation) we used Pearson's chi-square contingency tests to examine differences in the numbers of Maintain versus Improve allotments for which data were present. We then used contingency tests to compare data presence for Maintain and Improve allotments in the full sample of 310 allotments versus the subset failing due to livestock, for each of the four main data types (Actual use, Utilization, Trend, and Photo Point). Next, we used ANOVA to test for differences in percent data presence among those four data types. Our model included a main effect of data type (n=4), a block effect of field office (n=13), and their interaction. The response variable was the arcsin-transformed percent presence of each data type.

For LHS data, we used a split-block ANOVA design to test for differences between allotment categories (Maintain/Improve) and among data types (Upland, Riparian, Biodiversity). The model included state (for example, CO, UT, OR) as block, allotment category (Maintain/Improve) as subblock, data type as main treatment (Upland, Riparian, Biodiversity), and all 2-way interactions. The model was run twice, first with arcsin-transformed "percent of allotments meeting LHS" as the response variable, and second with arcsin-transformed "percent of allotments with unmet LHS attributed to livestock" as the response variable. In all cases, we used Tukey post-hoc tests.

Results

Field Office Sampling

Overall, more data were present for the 201 "Improve" than the 109 "Maintain" allotments we sampled, although differences were not significant (table 1; p>0.05). We found that, between 1997 and 2007, allotment files contained significantly more Actual Use (permittee-reported livestock number and season-of-use) data (59–77 percent) and repeat Photo Point data (53–61 percent) than quantitative Vegetation Trend data (34–38 percent), with forage Utilization present an intermediate amount (51–52 percent) (fig. 4; Tukey p<0.05). We also found that field offices varied significantly with respect to data availability ($F_{12,36}$=3.69, p=0.001).

Actual Use was reported in an average of 6–7 of the 11 years sampled (1997 to 2007) (table 1). Actual Use data were present for 59 percent of the 109 Maintain and 77 percent of the 201 Improve allotments (table 1), and availability of Actual Use data varied considerably across field offices. In addition, Actual Use data were not necessarily complete on an allotment in a given year, particularly on large multi-permittee allotments where all operators may not have reported numbers. (Similarly, Utilization, Photo Point, and vegetation cover data often were present only for a subset of pastures or key areas within a given allotment). In general, Billed Use information appeared to be a good predictor of Actual Use numbers (R^2=0.75, fig. 5).

Photo Points were the most commonly and frequently collected type of vegetation/soil monitoring data (fig. 4). Every Field Office we visited monitored with photo points, and 58 percent of allotments had photos taken at least once between 1997 and 2007 (table 1). Additionally, we observed that even those allotments with little or no photo data during this time period typically had early photo point dates in the 1960s, 1970s, and/or 1980s.

11

Utilization data were collected in more than one-half (52 percent) of allotments. All offices had collected Utilization data during our sample period, and all but one office used the Key Species method of making ocular utilization estimates (table 2). Quantitative Vegetation Trend data had been collected in 34–38 percent of allotments and by 10 of 13 offices, although approaches to data collection varied across offices (tables 1 and 2). Cover data were collected by 10 of 13 offices, with five different methods, and frequency data were collected by six offices, using three different methods (table 2).

We found that 26 percent of Improve allotments and 17 percent of Maintain allotments contained either grazing or allotment management plans that had been updated since 1997 (although an additional 35 and 29 percent, respectively, contained plans that had last been updated prior to 1997) (table 1). Few allotment evaluations of the objectives contained in those plans had been conducted in the previous 10 years for either Improve or Maintain allotments (15 and 8 percent, respectively, table 1).

Land Health Standards Data

The percentage of allotments with LHS evaluations completed between 1997 and 2007 was 57 percent, ranging from 22 to 95 percent, depending on state (table 3). Of the allotments with completed LHS evaluations (fig. 6), the BLM found 67 percent to be meeting all LHS, with "Maintain" allotments more commonly meeting standards than "Improve" allotments (table 3, fig. 6). Of all 5,991 allotments evaluated, 15 percent failed at least one standard due to livestock. Riparian standard failures were attributed to livestock significantly more (63 percent of cases) than were Upland or Biodiversity failures (52 and 46 percent, respectively) (table 3, Tukey $p<0.05$); this effect appears to have been driven largely by the failure of Riparian Improve allotments (significant standards * allotment status interaction, table 3). We found that the use of systematic rating systems of key indicators of rangeland health (for example, Pellant and others, 2005) varied across offices. Three offices did not use systematic indicator ratings, while nine did (and one is unknown).

Land Health Standards and Monitoring Data

We wanted to know which types of information could be used to support determinations that livestock were contributing to rangeland health issues. In our sampling of 310 allotments, we found that, when livestock were identified as the reason for not meeting a land health standard (n=62), Actual Use data (quantitative data on livestock number and season-of-use) were present for 47 percent of Maintain and 84 percent of Improve allotments (table 1). Forage utilization measurements had been made in one-half (52 percent) of allotments that did not meet standards due to livestock (table 1). Quantitative vegetation data were present for 35 percent of allotments failing due to livestock, although additional vegetation data could potentially be gleaned from photos at permanent photo plots, which were present for 69 percent of allotments (table 1). A full complement of monitoring data (four data types listed above and in table 1) was present for 27 percent of allotments (table 1). Overall, the amount of data associated with the 62 Maintain and Improve allotments failing standards due to livestock did not differ significantly from the full dataset of 310 allotments (Actual Use $\chi^2= 2.3$, p=0.1, Utilization $\chi^2=0.53$, p=0.5, Trend $\chi^2=0.25$, p=0.6, Photo Points $\chi^2=0.68$, p=0.4).

Expert Opinions

Overall, federal and university scientists expressed relatively similar opinions on our discussion topics (table 4). For data presentation, we separate our results for these two groups, but given our small sample sizes we did not attempt to analyze group differences statistically.

Ground cover (including vegetation, litter, rocks, biotic crusts and bare soil) was the variable most consistently identified by federal and university rangeland scientists (55 and 70 percent, respectively) as an important field measure for monitoring rangeland condition and livestock effects (table 4). Although measures of bare ground are implicit in some approaches to cover measurement/estimation, 45 percent of federal and 21 percent of university scientists who mentioned cover also specifically mentioned bare ground measurements, as did one other federal scientist (who had not specifically mentioned cover). Additionally, 5 percent of federal and university scientists mentioned gap measurements (which quantify the proportion of ground occupied by inter-plant gaps and provide information about potential for erosion). Overall, only 25 percent of federal and 10 percent of university scientists specifically mentioned soil measurements such as aggregate stability or compaction (but not including bare ground).

Utilization measures were suggested by 35 percent of federal and 25 percent of university scientists as a highest monitoring priority (with an additional 15 percent of university scientists mentioning utilization as a secondary measure). Methodological approaches included utilization cages (3 federal/2 university scientists), stubble height or residual biomass (4 federal/5 university), use pattern mapping (2 university), and height/weight calculations (1 university).

Thirty percent of federal and 40 percent of university scientists stressed the importance of having a reference for comparison when monitoring (table 4). These bases for comparison included ungrazed reference areas (cattle excluded) (4 federal/3 university), moderately grazed reference areas (3 university), and NRCS ecological site descriptions (3 federal/4 university).

Thirty percent of federal and 15 percent of university scientists recommended using repeat photo points as a primary approach to vegetation and soil monitoring (with an additional 15 percent of university mentioning it secondarily) (table 4). Approaches included traditional methods of returning regularly to fixed locations to take landscape and ground plot photos, as well as photo sampling along transects.

The use of remote sensing was suggested by 30 percent of federal and 35 percent of university scientists (table 4). Approaches included high resolution aerial photography (from airplane or lower flying remotely controlled device) and satellite imagery. In many of these cases, remote sensing was suggested as a tool for identifying risk and/or prioritizing monitoring activities. Overall, 25 percent of federal and 20 percent of university scientists mentioned the importance of using some type of tool or indicator (for example, remote sensing or other ground-based assessment) to prioritize monitoring.

Discussion

We found that BLM LHS evaluations, particularly with respect to determination of livestock grazing effects, would benefit from increased availability of monitoring data. This monitoring information, especially if collected with more consistent methodology, also would facilitate reporting of condition and trend of BLM rangelands and provide data-supported justification for management decisions. Rangeland experts emphasized the importance of continued efforts to monitor metrics of livestock use and vegetation trend, as well as collect climate data. Experts also suggested that monitoring programs could be refined to better prioritize monitoring locations and activities, capitalize on livestock operator involvement, and/or form specialized regional monitoring teams.

Land Health Standards

Since 1997, regulations have linked grazing practices on BLM land to the status of LHS; if an allotment fails LHS due to livestock, appropriate corrective action must be taken and the terms and conditions of the grazing permit may be adjusted (43 CFR 4180.2). In practice, this has meant that BLM has sought to complete LHS evaluations for allotments prior to permit renewal. Range-wide, however, both meeting of standards and the purported role of livestock varied considerably. Although these contrasting results likely reflect some true differences in grazing management across regions and/or field offices, they also likely reflect different approaches to evaluating and interpreting LHS (for example, use of systematic indicator ratings by only some of the offices). A more uniform and systematic approach to LHS data collection would likely maintain usefulness of the evaluation to individual field offices, but would greatly improve the reliability of the LHS dataset for making range-wide assessments of land health.

When a Land Health Standard is not met on a given allotment, the BLM must use additional information ("all available data") to determine whether livestock grazing is the cause (fig. 3). That is, the key indicators used to determine whether a standard is met do not provide information about causality. Rather, monitoring information such as livestock numbers, Utilization, Vegetation Trend, and Photo Point data should be used to help managers determine livestock causality. We found that collection of these types of data could be improved. Of the 62 allotments that failed LHS due to livestock, less than one-third (27 percent) possessed a full complement (all four data types) of monitoring data that could be used to quantitatively support the conclusion that livestock grazing contributed to poor land health. For 20 percent of the 62 allotments, none of the four data types existed. In cases when supporting data do not exist, although expert opinion (of BLM range staff) may provide accurate assessments of the effects of livestock grazing on an allotment, lack of quantitative long-term data makes grazing management decisions difficult to defend.

Actual Use and Utilization

Grazing intensity—including stocking rate, duration and frequency—has consistently been identified as having impacts on ecosystem and rangeland health (Vallentine, 1990; Briske and others, 2008). Similarly, the timing of grazing, particularly relative to plant phenology, can influence the sustainability of grazing (Briske and Richards, 1995). We found that grazing intensity and timing information (that is, Actual Use data) were present for 71 percent of the allotments and for an average of 6–7 of the 11 years between 1997 and 2007. The BLM typically sends Actual Use Forms to livestock operators (permittees) who must self-report livestock numbers and grazing dates. This Actual Use information greatly improves the ability of BLM to retrospectively examine the appropriateness of stocking rates and make official adjustments to allowable AUMs on a given allotment. Although annual adjustments can be negotiated between the assigned BLM staff and permittee, permanent adjustments to legal grazing amounts incur administrative costs and therefore may occur infrequently. The latter types of grazing adjustments may be increasingly necessary in the future. Although the potential effects of climate change on rangeland ecosystems are not clear, permitted grazing amounts may need to be re-evaluated to cope with altered climate patterns. Improved and continued efforts to send out forms and solicit responses, as well as ensure accuracy of these Actual Use reports would improve the quality of this critical grazing information.

Our comparison of Actual and Billed Use suggests that both under- and over-reporting occurs (fig. 5). In addition to a reluctance to report over-grazing, incorrect interpretation of grazing regulations may lead to a perceived disincentive to accurately report livestock numbers less than the legal maximum for fear that grazing privileges may be taken away and given to someone who will utilize them fully. In such cases, it may be prudent to positively reinforce behavior (for example, destocking) that recognizes benefits associated with rest and lowered stocking numbers. Nonetheless, in general, we found BLM billing records to be a relatively good predictor of Actual Use. Because billing records are kept for all allotments bureau-wide, billing information may be a useful tool for performing broad-scale analyses or comprehensively depicting approximate grazing intensity across the Western United States. Similarly, Permitted Use data (see Section I), which also exist for all allotments, theoretically represent maximum grazing, and a ratio of billed:permitted may serve as an index (actual:maximum) of grazing intensity.

Aside from examination of livestock numbers, measures of utilization (herbivory by animals) immediately following grazing periods can help determine if livestock are contributing to rangeland resource problems. We asked our rangeland experts to assume that Actual Use information would be collected in their range monitoring scenarios, but more than a one-third of the experts also recommended collection of Utilization data to make the causative link between rangeland condition and livestock effects. In our BLM office visits, we found that Utilization data were collected in more than one-half of the allotments we sampled, and 12 of 13 offices used ocular estimates of key species. Although this ocular estimate approach is a relatively quick source of information and appears to have been widely applied across the Bureau, the major disadvantage is that the key forage method typically provides information only for the most common forage species in a given area. If an area has been previously degraded, the most common species currently at that site may not necessarily be the preferred forage species or the dominant species expected under reference conditions described in the ecological site description. Thus, while utilization of more common, less-preferred key species may be monitored, use of less-common (but more preferred and appropriate to the site) species may exceed appropriate levels, eventually leading to declines. Rangeland experts suggested a number of other approaches to utilization, although in all cases highlighted significant drawbacks to the method. In general, measuring utilization can be problematic (Jasmer and Holechek, 1984).

Vegetation Trend

Ground cover was identified by 63 percent of rangeland experts as being one of the most important field measures for monitoring rangelands and livestock impacts. Cover measurements made by species, life-form, or functional group can provide important information about the health and functioning of the plant community and ecosystem properties (Herrick and others, 2005). Furthermore, many cover measurements include measurements of bare ground and total cover, with higher-than-normal bare ground typically reflecting increased potential for soil degradation. Basal gap measurements (mentioned by one federal and one university scientist) may be useful supplemental indicators of longer-term change (Herrick and others, 2005). Minimizing soil degradation is essential to maintaining rangeland health (Task Group on Unity in Concepts and Terminology Committee Members, 1995), and one-third of experts emphasized this point (that is, cited the importance of bare ground measurements). Any type of bare ground measurements, however, should be interpreted in the context of species cover data because bare ground can be negatively correlated with cover of undesirable invasive species.

Considering the importance placed upon cover measurements by our rangeland experts, increasing the frequency of cover measurements over time and across BLM allotments appears critical for monitoring rangeland condition. We found that cover data collection had occurred for only 37 percent of the allotments we examined and in those allotments had only been collected an average of one time between 1997 and 2007. Temporal cover information (collected over multiple years) coupled with annual growing season precipitation data provides information that can be used to evaluate trends in condition. Although 10 of the 13 BLM Field Offices we visited had collected cover data, methods of cover data collection varied across offices, making any potential comparisons or merging of datasets across regions difficult. Moving towards more consistent cover methodology—even within BLM districts—may aid landscape-scale management.

Another approach to assessing Vegetation Trend, collection of frequency data, was used by 6 of 13 BLM Offices. Although frequency data may be easier and faster to collect, it generally serves as a poor early warning indicator due to an inability to detect small changes in plant communities unless high levels of initial frequency have been previously recorded (Smith and others, 1986) and was mentioned by only one rangeland expert. Whereas cover methods can be used to indirectly detect declines in plant biomass, frequency methods are more likely to detect changes associated with plant mortality (Elzinga and others, 2001b); once significant mortality has occurred recovery of smaller populations of less vigorous individuals is more problematic. Frequency methods can be used to complement cover methods and for example may be especially helpful for monitoring spread of undesirable species (Elzinga and others, 2001b), although this approach would require implementing and repeating two techniques.

For specific plant species or functional groups (for example, rare plants, invasive species, woody species), additional methods may be necessary to best assess their status and make predictions about future distributions. Accordingly, BLM Field Offices typically measure these in separate studies. Monitoring of these plant groups may be especially important as they can be important correlates of other variables (for example, invasive species and native plant cover) (Anderson and Inouye, 2001). Additionally, general vegetation monitoring programs may benefit from the addition of assessments of spatial cover distributions to capture patchiness and spatial processes in plant communities and make predictions about future cover.

Repeat Photos

Thirty percent of experts recommended photo sampling. At a given photo point, pictures can be taken of an overhead view of a small (for example, 1 ×1 m) permanent plot as well as of a landscape view, and this procedure can be repeated over time to detect large changes in vegetation (Elzinga and others, 2001b; Herrick and others, 2001). Overhead photos can be used to track bare ground and cover by functional groups, and in the cases of larger plants, individual species. Landscape photos provide insight into not only the general appearance of the landscape, but changes in woody species. Experts also recommended modified photo methods for more intensive sampling. For example multiple overhead photos can be taken along transects, or high resolution panoramic images could be incorporated into sampling (for example, Nichols and others, 2009).

An appeal to a photo sampling approach is that it is a quick inexpensive field method that requires little training, and qualitative or quantitative analyses of the photos can be delayed and performed in the office at a later time. One expert also suggested that photo points are the most compelling evidence in court cases for illustrating vegetation trends to people who lack rangeland expertise or are unfamiliar with data interpretation.

According to our BLM data survey, photo points were the most common and frequently collected (in 58 percent of allotments) vegetation monitoring data. Even those allotments with little or no photo data during this time period typically had early photo point dates in the 1960s, 1970s, and/or 1980s. Overall, BLM photo point data appear to represent the most complete historic vegetation information, spanning the longest time period. Continued and increased efforts to repeat photos would be inexpensive, promote time spent in the field, and provide one type of continuous long-term information about vegetation change on BLM allotments.

Reference Areas and Climate

We did not systematically assess use of reference areas by BLM, but 35 percent of experts expressed support for use of reference areas when assessing livestock impacts. Ideas included completely ungrazed areas (for example, exclosures, highway rights-of-way, or far from water points), grazing gradients (for example, different distances from water points), and use of reference state community descriptions in NRCS Ecological Site Descriptions (ESD). Some approaches, such as building and maintaining exclosures can be expensive, whereas other approaches, such as using existing NRCS ESD data would be more cost-efficient and practical. Accordingly, the Interpreting Indicators of Rangeland Health technique changed from using reference areas to using ESD data because of difficulties in finding appropriate reference areas (Pyke and others, 2002). When feasible, however, pairing a particular site with a similar nearby reference site would be useful.

When using reference communities, considerations for interpretation of results include: choice of reference community (for example, historical vegetation versus more recent, grazed versus ungrazed), impacts of wild ungulates, and how long-term herbivore exclusion might alter vegetation-soil dynamics. Use of reference areas may be especially important when considering the dramatic yearly variations in climate and weather and the effects of those variations on plants, soils and their relationships with grazing.

Climate and weather data, particularly rainfall patterns that can exhibit dramatic inter- and intra-annual variation, provide necessary context for interpreting vegetation and livestock monitoring information. For instance, yearly rainfall amounts have direct bearing on the impacts of a given grazing intensity (Thurow and Taylor, 1999), and the timing of grazing relative to rainfall (and phenology) also determines overall grazing effects (Briske and Richards, 1995). Likewise, any long-term trends in vegetation cover would be strongly affected by lengthy drought periods, both with and without grazing. Although we did not specifically sample for the availability of climate information at BLM offices, climate and weather station data are supposed to be included within their monitoring programs. Inclusion of their own climate data in grazing files, as well as data regularly retrieved from other sources (for example, NOAA), would aid interpretation of monitoring data. For example, plotting long-term actual use numbers relative to growing season precipitation values could help guide stocking rate decisions. Similarly, assessments of these types of long-term relationships could provide insights into how rangelands might respond to pending climate change.

Prioritization of Monitoring Efforts

Given the vast land area administered by the BLM and time constraints associated with monitoring activities, prioritization of where and when to monitor is essential. Although we found that allotments BLM classified as "Improve" were more likely to have failed standards due to livestock, we did not find significantly more monitoring data for Improve allotments. This suggests a need for further efforts at prioritization.

Currently, monitoring efforts focus largely on key areas. These areas were established as representative of larger areas (for example, pastures or allotments) and contained dominant forage plants for livestock grazing. Although current monitoring also includes critical areas, BLM may benefit from further emphasis on critical or at-risk areas rather than key areas. Twenty-three percent of the experts we interviewed specifically mentioned identification of high-risk areas for concentration of monitoring efforts. For example, identifying areas that appear to be at or near thresholds of change (in a state-and-transition framework) may be a cost effective approach to identifying areas where management actions are sufficient to sustain or improve range condition (Bestelmeyer, 2006). Approaches include use of on-the-ground indicators (for example, bareground, vegetation gaps, and biotic crusts which are sensitive to grazing), Geographic Information Systems (for example, combine known stocking rates with information on ecological sites that may be more vulnerable or less resilient to grazing, see Section I) and remote sensing (see Section III and Homer and others, *in press*). A major benefit of the latter is that it can be used at multiple scales. For instance, satellite imagery can be used at the broadest scales as a primary indicator (for example, production and rainfall/drought effects across a region). Satellite imagery and/or high resolution aerial photographs also can be used at the landscape scale to assess ecosystem properties that have implications for wildlife and land health, such as bare ground or woody plant cover and structure (Booth and Cox, 2008; Rango and others, 2009; Homer and others, *in press*). At this scale, it may be possible to identify indicators of thresholds where more intensive monitoring efforts should be concentrated (see Xian and others, *in press*; Homer and others, *in press*; Section III, this report), and even use remote sensing to monitor changes in rangeland health conditions (see Xian and others, *in press*; Section III, this report).

Increased Involvement of Livestock Operators

In addition to helping maintain genial BLM-permittee relationships, increased involvement of livestock operators in the monitoring process could provide useful complementary monitoring data. First, as discussed above, permittee reporting of livestock numbers and grazing dates could be refined to be more complete and accurate and therefore provide a better picture of grazing intensity on BLM land. Second, as two experts recommended, livestock in-out weights or end-of-season body condition scores could provide insight into forage conditions. This type of information is of clear use to the permittee, and for BLM, would provide information to complement Utilization or Vegetation Trend numbers. Third, permittees may be interested in maintaining livestock exclosures as reference areas. Fourth, permittees could be more involved in collecting all types of BLM monitoring, from easier tasks such as reporting rain gauge readings on their allotments to more difficult tasks such as helping collect Vegetation Trend data. Although motivation and interest in participation are likely to vary considerably among permittees, local knowledge supplied by permittees has the potential to play a critical role in rangeland monitoring (for example, Bestelmeyer and others, 2009).

Monitoring Teams

A potential impediment to success of most of the above monitoring approaches is a lack of calibration and practice with the methods (for example, visual cover, production or utilization estimates, species identification). Similarly, monitoring may be hampered by an inability to visit field sites, particularly at the same time each year. One possibility for alleviating these types of problems is to designate field monitoring teams that cover wide geographical areas. One example suggested by a university rangeland expert was to create state- or regional-level teams that monitor long-term variables less frequently (for example, every 5 years). Workloads could be staggered so that multiple monitoring techniques could be applied to a given land area over time, but each technique would not necessarily be applied in a given year, nor all land areas monitored. Potential advantages include increased expertise and practice with monitoring techniques, insurance that either the method or decision-making process for deciding among a suite of methods is consistent across sites and time. A potential model for the monitoring team approach is the Utah Division of Wildlife Resources Range Trend Project, which hires seasonal technicians to collect yearly trend data at designated key areas throughout the State (http://wildlife.utah.gov/range/).

Employing a State- or regional-level team need not release range conservationists from the responsibility of visiting the field or collecting short-term data (for example, Utilization, Actual Use). Whereas the numbers collected by the monitoring team could provide a solid scientific justification for management decisions, range conservationists could spend time in the field making their own qualitative observations and short-term data measurements. Regardless of whether special monitoring teams are used in the future, prioritization of monitoring visits by the assigned range conservationist would still be beneficial. Several range scientists emphasized a need to maintain the 'art' of range management and the freedom to apply adaptive management.

Conclusions

In monitoring programs it is important to maintain continuity, use consistent methodology over time, and take into account all historical data to examine long-term trends. Several methods used by BLM were among those suggested by our conversations with rangeland experts (for example, photo points, point-sampling of vegetation). This suggests that those methods with the greatest support could be emphasized and potentially expanded on for the future. When we presented a hypothetical scenario to the university and federal rangeland science experts and asked them prioritize monitoring activities, the most common response was to measure ground/vegetation cover, a variable that in many cases (10 of 13 offices sampled) BLM had already identified as a monitoring priority. Although monitoring data were scant over our sample period, existing cover data nonetheless could serve as a basis for designing future monitoring efforts and be used for examination of long-term trends. Moreover, those areas where Vegetation Trend data are lacking altogether may present an opportunity to revise and produce protocols for more standardized field measures for future broader-scale analyses.

Because monitoring approaches vary so greatly across time and space, it may be necessary to introduce alternative approaches to effectively monitor at scales broader than individual management units. Effective management may not necessarily require that methods be uniform across allotments or regions. However, consistency of monitoring approaches across allotments or regions, along with collection of local-level data that are amenable to broader-scale analyses, are critical for issues such as conservation and maintenance of ecosystem services that transcend field office and political boundaries. Because travel time to and from management units is one of the more prohibitive aspects of monitoring, it may be reasonable to both continue previous methods (particularly important when consistent and abundant historic data exist) and add new methods to achieve more uniformity across management units. Several handbooks, guides and research programs already exist to guide monitoring efforts (for example, Bureau of Land Management, 1999; Elzinga and others, 2001a; Herrick and others, 2009; U.S. Department of Agriculture, Natural Resources Conservation Service, 2009c). Collaborations between research and management could produce quantitative models for making transitions from former to newer techniques, allowing for continuity of Vegetation Trend data and eventually leading to elimination of methodological overlaps. However, to achieve consistency, either across allotments or within allotments over time, will require decisions and greater guidance from levels above individual BLM field offices.

BLM faces significant obstacles for maintaining monitoring programs, particularly lack of time, labor, and prioritization (West, 2003). In addition to the time necessary to perform monitoring tasks, many monitoring methods must be performed at the same time every year, which can be problematic when a single range conservationist is assigned to multiple allotments. The most efficient and realistic monitoring approaches may include some more comprehensive and labor-intensive methods to track and evaluate long-term trends (for example, gaps or species composition). These methods could be carried out less frequently, be completed by special monitoring teams, or use photo or remote-sensing approaches that allow data processing at other times of year. Results could then be viewed in the context of potentially less field-intensive yearly monitoring (for example, Utilization, Actual Use) that is done more frequently, potentially with some assistance from permittees. In the absence of further funding or added personnel, strictly prioritizing field monitoring activities for a given time period each year is the most critical step towards achieving the most effective monitoring.

Section III: Exploring Relationships among Livestock Grazing, Land Health Standards, and Remotely Sensed Vegetation Characteristics

Introduction

The impacts of livestock grazing in sagebrush steppe, one of the largest biomes in North America, are difficult to measure, but are critical to understanding and determining sound land management practices across the West. Although appropriate grazing practices may be sustainable and compatible with conservation, inappropriate livestock grazing can alter species composition of communities, disrupt ecosystem function, and alter ecosystem structure (Dyksterhuis, 1949). Quantitative measures are needed to adequately assess grazing impacts and offer insight into improved land management, especially in the face of global change. Understanding the impacts of current grazing practices as well as identifying where habitats may be at risk is crucial to the persistence of sagebrush habitats and the species which rely on them (Aldridge and others, 2008).

Greater Sage-Grouse (*Centocercus urophasianus*) are a landscape species occurring across a broad range of sagebrush habitats throughout the West (Schroeder and others, 2004). Recently, the U.S. Fish and Wildlife Service ruled that the species was warranted for listing under the Endangered Species Act (Federal Register, 2010) but precluded by higher priority listing actions. Understanding risks associated with grazing practices across the range of this species will allow for conservation measures which ensure the persistence of this and other sagebrush obligates. Long-term monitoring programs which provide an accurate assessment of the impacts of grazing on the sagebrush ecosystem will enable land managers to assess how grazing effects landscape change. Current monitoring data regarding these impacts are not available in a form useful for relating to sage-grouse populations (Miller and others, 2011).

In the Western United States, approximately one-half of remaining sagebrush steppe is public grazing land. One of the major public land management agencies, the Bureau of Land Management (BLM), manages its grazing program using an allotment-based approach. A grazing allotment is defined as an area of land designated and managed for livestock grazing (Bureau of Land Management, 2001) and consists of an area of land with boundaries based on a variety of factors such as land ownership, topography, and State boundaries (see fig. 6). Most data for monitoring livestock grazing and its effects, such as assessments of Land Health Standards (LHS), are collected by BLM and recorded for individual allotments (Bureau of Land Management, 2001). Ideally, LHS address rangeland health, defined as the degree to which the integrity of the soil and ecological processes are functioning properly to maintain the structure, organization and activity of the system over time (Bureau of Land Management, 2001). Land Health Standards are assessed by BLM on an approximate 10-year cycle by allotment, and allotments can fail to meet LHS for various reasons such as impacts from wildfire, invasive species, drought, or off-highway vehicle (OHV) use. In cases where current grazing management is identified as a significant causal factor contributing to unmet LHS, changes to the grazing regime are required to be implemented by the subsequent grazing season.

The results of LHS assessments across multiple allotments could be used to depict rangeland health across a broader landscape. Up to this point, however, this has been difficult, as a comprehensive geographic dataset has not been previously available. Additionally, combining high resolution vegetation maps derived from remotely-sensed data (Homer and others, 2008; Homer and others, *in press*) with LHS data collected at the allotment level may yield important application to on-the-ground management and provide the BLM with tools to identify "at risk" habitats. Similar tools are already being used to monitor habitat changes over time (Xian and others, *in press*). Although these remotely sensed products offer great opportunities to enhance much-needed long-term monitoring (see Xian and others, *in press*), understanding potential mechanisms related to these changes also could provide managers with more insights into management of sagebrush ecosystems. Assessing the relationship between vegetation characteristics and rangeland health assessments across large spatial extents would help aid land managers with understanding consequences of management actions.

Our overall goal was to show how these allotment data can be used in an applied management context, directly assisting BLM with management activities. More specifically, we were interested in testing if high resolution vegetation maps derived from remotely sensed imagery (Homer and others, 2008; Homer and others, *in press*),could be used as a tool to help identify allotments where rangeland health has been degraded, and if differences in characteristics could be discerned in allotments where current livestock management practices are indicated as the cause. If so, these products may be useful as landscape-level rangeland monitoring and management tools. We predict that allotments where LHS are "Not met"will have more bare ground, less shrub cover, and less vegetation (herbaceous and litter) cover. Similarly, we predict that where livestock are responsible for the failure to meet standards, these allotments will have more bare ground and less herbaceous and litter cover based on knowledge that cattle and sheep have grazing preferences for herbaceous forage and tend to treat shrubs (browse) as undesirable (Stoddart and others, 1995) or poisonous as in the case of big sagebrush (Johnson and others, 1976).

Methods

Datasets and Spatial Compilation

We used spatial allotment data compiled as part of this larger project (see Section I of this report) and joined it with tabular data on LHS synthesized previously and described in Section I. Our LHS synthesis classified each allotment as having "Met" (if it met Upland, Riparian, and Biodiversity standards) or "Not met" (if it failed to meet at least one standard). Appendixes 1 and 2 detail the procedure used in the identification and refinement of the spatial allotment data and LHS, respectively.

Recently, products mapping estimated percent cover of sagebrush rangeland vegetation characteristics were developed, using fractional vegetation predictions to calculate cover percentage values within individual 30 m pixels (see Homer and others, 2008; Homer and others, *in press*). These map products have been completed for sagebrush habitats across Wyoming (sampled in 2006–07), within the Gunnison Basin of Colorado (sampled in 2007), and for the area covered by the Billings, Montana BLM Field Office (sampled in 2008). Model application varied slightly across sites, but all followed the same field sampling protocols and modeling processes using similar remotely sensed imagery to model eight main rangeland vegetation components; see Homer and others (2008) and Homer and others (*in press*) for details. Here, we utilize four products to make comparison across allotments: percent cover of sagebrush (all species combined), herbaceous vegetation, litter, and bare soil. For each individual allotment, we summarized per-pixel cover estimates across all pixels within that allotment. To do this, we calculated the mean and median estimated percent cover across all pixels, assessing overall vegetation or bare ground cover within an allotment. However, activities that affect the rangeland health assessment of an allotment, also may affect the heterogeneity of vegetation cover within an allotment (for example, Adler and others, 2001).Thus, we also calculated the standard deviation of per-pixel cover values across all pixels within each allotment, providing an estimate of heterogeneity for each variable of interest. All summarized allotment values (means, medians, or standard deviation) were calculated using a zonal statistic in ArcGIS 9.3.1 (ESRI, Redlands, CA, USA). These mean, median, and standard deviation values for each allotment were used to compare vegetation characteristics across LHS classes. Any allotment that was not within the extent of the sagebrush map data was omitted from the analysis.

Statistical Analyses

Initially, we conducted simple comparisons using a two-tailed t-test with unequal variances to compare mean differences in rangeland variables for each comparison of interest. These included first contrasting "Not met" (1) versus "Met" (0) allotments, and then contrasting when "Not met" were deemed to have been caused by livestock (1) versus 'other' causes (0). BLM is only required to specify causal factors of failure when livestock are deemed responsible. To further assess our ability to predict the probability of a given allotment failing a LHS Assessment, we developed logistic regression models (Hosmer and Lemeshow, 2000) using different combinations of sagebrush rangeland vegetation characteristics within a given allotment to predict LHS failure.

Model Development

We included 'state' as a fixed effect with the most prevalent State (Wyoming) as the reference category to account for any inherent state-level difference in LHS assessments. Clearly, many of our metrics (mean, median, or standard deviation) within each variable class (cover of sagebrush, herbaceous, litter, bare) could be highly correlated. Thus, for both analyses, we initially assessed each individual metric and combinations (mean or median each with standard deviation) for each variable subgroup in a separate analysis to identify the most predictive form of each variable. This resulted in four subgroup analyses, each consisting of five different models. The most predictive subgroup model based on Akaike's Information Criterion corrected for small sample sizes (AIC_c; Burnham and Anderson, 2002) was carried forward for the development of candidate models considering all four top subgroup model forms for model building. Correlated variables (Pearson's $r \geq |0.7|$) were prevented from occurring in the same model. Combined candidate models were again assessed and ranked using AIC_c.

Model Evaluation

Ideally, we would challenge our models with an independent set of data to evaluate the ability of our model(s) to predict LHS failure. Given the limited data available at this time on LHS assessments, we chose not to fold our data into training and testing datasets, as is common practice. Thus, for both models, we only present within sample assessment of model predictions. We used a Hosmer and Lemeshow χ^2 goodness of fit test (Hosmer and Lemeshow, 2000) to assess model fit to the data and receiver operating characteristic (ROC) curves to estimate predictive accuracy (Fielding and Bell, 1997). ROC values greater than 0.9 have high model accuracy, 0.7–0.9 good model accuracy, and < 0.7 low model accuracy (Swets, 1988; Manel and others, 2001). We identified the optimal probability classification point for each final model by minimizing the absolute value of the difference between sensitivity and specificity curves (Liu and others, 2005). We estimated the model's overall predictive classification accuracy at the identified classification point using percentage correctly classified (PCC), and considered scores of ≥ 70 percent to have reasonable prediction and ≥ 80 percent excellent prediction (Nielsen and others, 2004; Aldridge and Boyce, 2007).

Spatial Application and Multi-Model Inference

For both modeling approaches, we considered all models from the candidate set within 2 AIC_c points of the top model to have strong support, and used model averaging over this set to produce more robust spatial predictions and strengthen inference (Burnham and Anderson, 2002). When necessary, prior to applying the adjusted weights to the spatial prediction for each model across all allotments, we rescaled model weights to sum to 1, only considering models within the 2 AIC_c model set. Weighted predictions were then added together to produce a final probability of LHS failure surface. We first applied the probability of failure ("Not met" versus "Met") model to all allotments across our three study areas where we had spatial data, regardless of whether LHS had previously been assessed. We then used the optimal classification point (see above) to classify all allotments into "Met" or "Not met" status. The second model predicting the risk of failure due to livestock compared to 'other' failures was subsequently only applied to allotments having previously been predicted to have "Not met" (first analysis).

Results

Comparison Across Allotment Status

Our final dataset with LHS information and sagebrush rangeland vegetation characteristics consisted of 798 allotments that met and 333 allotments that did not meet LHS. Allotments that met LHS had different sagebrush rangeland vegetation characteristics than those that did not meet LHS (table 5). Generally, allotments that met LHS had significantly greater cover of sagebrush (9.8versus 8.2 percent), herbaceous vegetation (24.3 versus 18.2 percent), and litter (21.0 versus 18.2 percent), but significantly lower cover of exposed bare soil (42.7 versus 52.4 percent; table 5). Heterogeneity in cover for all four variables (standard deviation of pixels within allotments) decreased for those that did not meet LHS, but was not significant for bare soil (table 5).

Livestock were identified as the reason for unmet standards for 132 of the 333 allotments that did not met standards. Compared to other allotments, allotments where unmet standards were attributed to livestock had more cover of sagebrush (9.0 versus 7.6 percent), herbaceous vegetation (20.1 versus 17.0 percent) and litter (19.5 versus 17.4 percent), but less exposed bare soil (48.6 versus 54.8 percent; table 6). Variability in cover (standard deviation) was greater where livestock were deemed the cause across all four cover variables, though not significant for herbaceous (table 6).

"Met-"Not Met" Models

State-level differences were inherent in the logistic regression analyses comparing "Met" versus "Not met" allotments. Thus, all further models included 'state' as a fixed effect. Top metrics for each variable subgroup included mean cover of sagebrush (sb_mean), mean litter cover (lt_mean), herbaceous cover and variability (hb_mean + hb_std), and bare soil and variability (ba_mean + ba_std; table 7). These top four subgroup models were carried forward for development of candidate models using all combinations of models. Bare soil (mean) was inversely correlated with mean herbaceous cover and mean litter cover, resulting in a total seven combined candidate models (table 8). The top AIC_c-selected failure model predicted that LHS-failed pastures have less sagebrush cover ($\beta_{sb\text{-}mean}$ = -0.118), less cover of herbaceous vegetation ($\beta_{hb\text{-}mean}$ = -0.065), but more variability in herbaceous cover ($\beta_{hb\text{-}std}$ = 0.044, table 9). Relative to Wyoming, Colorado ($\beta_{state\text{-}1}$ = 3.468) had higher rates of failing to meet standards, whereas rates of allotments having "Not met" standards were slightly lower in Billings, MT ($\beta_{state\text{-}2}$ = -0.146, table 9).

This top "Met"-"Not met" model had strong support with a high weight of evidence given our final candidate set of models (w_i = 1.0, table 8), and was used for spatial modeling. This model had reasonable fit to the data (H-L χ_8^2 = 13.35, P = 0.10) and good model accuracy (ROC = 0.722). Although variance explained for this relatively simply model was reasonable (pseudo-R^2 =13.24 percent), overall prediction based on the optimal classification point (0.271) was low (PCC = 65.61 percent).

"Livestock" Versus "Other" Models

State was again used as a fixed effect for logistic regression analyses comparing allotments where unmet standards were attributed to "livestock" versus "other" reasons. Top metrics for each variable subgroup included cover of sagebrush (sb_mean), variability of litter cover alone (lt_std), herbaceous cover (hb_mean), and cover and variability of bare soil (ba_mean + ba_std; table 10). All these four top subgroup models were used for combined candidate modeling of all combinations; mean bare soil cover was inversely correlated with herbaceous cover, and these two variables were not considered together, resulting in 10 candidate models (Ttble 11). Two models had reasonable support within the candidate set (table 11). The top AIC_c-selected model ($w_i = 0.416$, table 11) predicted that "livestock" allotments had more sagebrush cover than "other" allotments ($\beta_{sb\text{-}mean} = 0.084$), with a weaker effect of less bare soil ($\beta_{ba\text{-}mean} = -0.005$) but stronger effect of increased variability in bare soil cover ($\beta_{ba\text{-}std} = 0.096$, table 12). Both Colorado ($\beta_{state\text{-}1} = 1.154$) and Montana ($\beta_{state\text{-}2} = 0.952$ table 12) sites had higher rates of unmet standards due to livestock relative to Wyoming. The second model had moderate support ($w_i = 0.255$, table 11), and differed only in the addition of mean litter cover to the model, predicting less litter in "livestock" allotments ($\beta_{lt\text{-}mean} = -0.109$, table 12), although the effect was very weak (SE = 0.100, table 12). Magnitude and direction of responses to other metrics in this second model were similar to that of the top model (see table 12).

The top "livestock" model had good fit to the data (H-L $\chi_8^2 = 5.52$, $P = 0.700$), but low model accuracy (ROC = 0.688). The second ranked model had similar fit (H-L $\chi_8^2 = 5.06$, $P = 0.751$) and accuracy (ROC = 0.693). Variance explained for the top and second models was reasonable (pseudo-$R^2 = 7.81$ and 8.08 percent, respectively). Combining these two top models to generate an overall model averaged prediction resulted in similar model accuracy (ROC = 0.690) and prediction (PCC = 62.67 percent) based on the optimal classification point (0.398).

Spatial Application

Despite the moderate to low model accuracy and prediction success for these two relatively simply models, we felt it was useful to develop spatial applications of these models, to (1) illustrate the application of these datasets for aiding in management, and (2) directly help with identification of areas that could be considered for more local rangeland management assessments and management priorities. When applied spatially to all 3,564 allotments where we had sagebrush rangeland vegetation characteristics, our model predicts that 1,510 (about 42 percent) are at risk of not meeting LHS (fig. 7). The majority of these occur in northwestern Wyoming into the south-central portions of the Billings MT BLM Field Office, southwestern Wyoming, and across all allotments in the Gunnison Basin, Colorado (fig. 7). Conversely, when the reason for not meeting standards was considered, risk of failing to meet standards due to livestock was the greatest for allotments in central Wyoming, central southwestern Wyoming, most of the allotments not meeting standards in Billing, Montana, and all allotments not meeting standards in Gunnison, Colorado (ig. 8). Although we show risk of failure to meet standards due to livestock as a continuous probability surface (fig. 8), using the optimal classification point 446 of the 1,510 failed allotments (about 30 percent) are predicted to have not met standards, with livestock as the primary cause.

Discussion

We conducted a relatively simple comparison of vegetation characteristics across grazing allotments, contrasting allotments that have "Met" versus "Not met" LHS. We had a unique opportunity to use recently developed remotely sensed vegetation classifications (Homer and others, *in press*) and the spatial grazing assessment information compiled for this project. Allotments that did not meet LHS had more bare ground, but less sagebrush, litter, and herbaceous vegetation, as predicted (table 5). The top AIC_c-identified spatial model (tables 8 and 9) indicated that "Not met" allotments were best differentiated from "Met" allotments based on lower amounts of sagebrush cover, less herbaceous cover, and a higher variability of herbaceous cover. Bare ground also was greater in allotments that had not met LHS, although it had a strong inverse correlation with herbaceous cover and was not included in the top candidate model. Following are potential explanations for these patterns.

First, loss of sagebrush cover can constitute a loss or reduction in dominance of a major structural plant group and thus contribute to departures from expected LHS (Pyke and others, 2002). Similarly, because wildlife can be strongly influenced by changes in vegetation structure decreased sagebrush cover may contribute to failure to meet wildlife-related standards. In our sampling area, loss of sagebrush cover commonly occurs following wildfire. Second, it is not surprising that allotments with decreased herbaceous cover were more likely to fail LHS because ground cover is a key predictor of plant community and ecosystem health and functioning (Herrick and others, 2005). Likewise, minimizing soil degradation (associated with bare ground) is at the basis of maintaining ecosystem health (Task group on unity in concepts and terminology committee members, 1995). Third, although overall herbaceous cover might be higher in some disturbed areas due to cheatgrass, high variability in herbaceous cover also is likely associated with disturbances and land uses that would cause an allotment to fail LHS. For example, mining activity or heavy grazing may occur in concentrated areas within an allotment (for example, mine site, or near water points), decreasing herbaceous cover relative to the rest of the landscape. Allotments receiving light use may appear more homogeneous.

We predicted that when livestock are responsible for unmet standards, those allotments will have more bare ground and less litter and herbaceous cover. Contrary to our predictions, on average, allotments where standards were unmet due to livestock had less bare ground (about 6 percent), more herbaceous cover (about 3 percent), and more litter (about 2 percent) than other allotments (table 6). Our top two AIC_c-selected models both suggested that "livestock" allotments had more sagebrush and slightly less bare ground, with more variability in bare ground cover than "other" allotments (table 12). Although the second model suggested there was less litter in "livestock" allotments, this was a very weak effect (see table 12). These patterns may be partially explained by other factors (aside from livestock grazing) that contribute to failure to meet LHS. For example drought, OHV use or recent fires likely create more intense disturbances than livestock; these more intense disturbances would be associated with increased bare ground and decreased herbaceous and shrub cover, and in some cases, decreased litter. When more intense land uses are present, the relative impacts of livestock grazing may be minimal, or the area may pass a threshold of degradation, such that it is no longer suitable for livestock grazing (and unmet standards are not attributable to livestock). Other factors BLM cited as contributing to unmet standards include but are not limited to: energy development, timber harvest, historical mining, road development, woody species encroachment, fire suppression, past effects of livestock grazing, weeds, non-native species invasions, recreation, wild horses, and wildlife (K.Veblen, personal observation).

Although the strength of our models could be improved, there also were several limitations to this initial analysis that ultimately reduced our ability to detect patterns and trends. BLM grazing data were incomplete in many cases (see Section II), and BLM record numbers for spatial and tabular data did not always match, limiting our sample sizes. Additionally, LHS assessments were conducted over an 11-year period (1997–2007), and vegetation models and remotely sensed imagery were static (over 1 or 2 years, depending on area). Our results probably also were weakened by the fact that vegetation characteristics could not be summarized for the specific portion of the allotment that resulted in the 'failing' assessment, and instead were summarized across entire allotments, some portions of which were probably 'healthy.' Current efforts are underway by BLM to investigate whether conducting LHS assessments for individual parcels within allotments will provide a more accurate picture of overall land health status (S. Karl, written commun., Bureau of Land Management, 2010). Despite the limitations to our approach, patterns in sagebrush vegetation components were still evident across "Not met" versus "Met" allotments, and to a lesser extent, between allotments where standards were unmet due to livestock versus other reasons.

We see potential in using the spatial predictions from our analyses as a management tool. In Section II of this report we found that 20 percent of federal and 25 percent of university rangeland science experts identified a need for monitoring prioritization tools, and 30 and 35 percent, respectively, specifically cited the utility of using remote-sensing approaches. Agencies such as the BLM, could spatially prioritize areas/allotments based on our predicted risk of failing to meet standards (figs. 7 and 8), identifying allotments most at risk of degraded rangeland conditions, especially given that only 1,131 of 3,564 (about 31 percent) of allotments in these three regions have been assessed between 1997 and 2007. Our model predicts that 1,510 of these allotments are at risk of not meeting LHS. Of the 2,433 allotments which had not yet had LHS assessments conducted as of 2007, our model predicts that 1,018 of these (about 42 percent) are at risk of not meeting LHS. This model and map (fig. 7) may provide a decision support tool to aid in the allocation of limited resources, prioritizing future assessments and management actions in areas of greatest concern (that is, highest risk of failure). For instance, our models predict a large number of unmet standards occurring in the Worland Basin in northeast Wyoming, and south of Kemmerer in southwest Wyoming, as well as across all available allotments in the Gunnison Basin (fig. 7). Although most of these allotments with available data in the Gunnison Basin, Colorado, were assessed and subsequently identified as allotments that did not meet standards (29 of 31), management efforts could focus on understanding potential causes of unmet standards in these areas in Wyoming and Colorado. Obviously, this does not alleviate the need to confirm the predictive capacity of these models, evaluating some allotments where our model predicts both met and unmet LHS. Ultimately, our model should be challenged with independent data, possibly by using ongoing LHS assessments by BLM (post-2007) or by using standardized LHS assessments conducted by an independent team of range ecologists in the field.

We believe that this initial application of allotment data illustrates the utility of both the grazing allotment data compiled in this report and the new remotely sensed vegetation classifications (Homer and others, 2008; Homer and others, *in press*), allowing for applied questions to be asked related to the monitoring and management of healthy sagebrush ecosystems. Our models could be improved by more complete (post-2007) coverage of LHS data. Field offices typically prioritize monitoring efforts in problem allotments (see Section II); thus, in districts or offices where a limited number of LHS assessments had been conducted, the sample may have been biased towards those less likely to meet LHS. For example, it is not clear whether Colorado showed lower rates of meeting standards relative to other States due to real differences in livestock management, more conservative LHS assessments, or a sample biased towards only conducting assessments in problem allotments. Our models also could be improved with the addition of other ancillary data, such as soils or ecological site information, as well as simple topographic information, such as digital elevation models or terrain indices. For example, addition of ecological site data might help explain why certain allotments were identified as higher risk than others in our maps and distinguish ecological from managerial causes. Additionally, the identification of specific locations within allotments where LHS are not being met, would allow for more robust models to be developed based on site-specific information, rather than averaging conditions across an entire allotment, improving model prediction. Finally, both the robustness of range-wide analyses and utility of this tool for managers would benefit from better standardization of LHS protocols. It would also be helpful to have finer resolution of which areas within allotments are failing to meet standards because an individual allotment typically is comprised of a multitude of ecological sites that vary in the types and amounts of vegetation independently of land use. As discussed in Section II of this report, LHS assessment protocols were not necessarily standardized across State or Office boundaries.

Our models and 'risk' maps could currently be used as initial grazing management tools, even though limitations exist. This application illustrates potential (if these limitations were addressed) to use these grazing datasets to ask future questions about how grazing activities might alter sagebrush ecosystem components across large landscapes, the potential consequences for associated species of concern, such as Greater Sage-Grouse, and ultimately, provide understanding of these system interactions to allow for improved management, where needed. In the future, information contained in these spatial datasets on LHS or changes in livestock use over time could be used to assess potential consequences of changes for wildlife populations; for example, temporal sage-grouse lek dynamics (Fedy and Aldridge, *in press*), or impacts to long-term changes in vegetation characteristics (Xian and others, *in press*), using time-series analyses of vegetation and/or temporal shifts in climate within these systems.

Conclusions

This project represents a first attempt to compile local-level, livestock grazing-related monitoring data from the BLM for the purpose of spatially analyzing broad-scale patterns in vegetation characteristics in sagebrush steppe habitat. This type of landscape level assessment would help inform future adaptive management of landscape level species such as Greater Sage-Grouse, especially in the context of multiple use management and climate change. Prior to our work, although local-level monitoring data existed, the data had not yet been critically evaluated for suitability in range-wide analyses, nor had there been any attempts to use it for such analyses. In general, we found that more consistent data collection methodologies across local-level (field) offices might improve the suitability of data for broad-scale analyses. We also did not find any local-level (on-the-ground) monitoring data (Actual Use, Utilization, Vegetation Trend) that had been collected consistently enough over time and space for range-wide, or even state-wide, analyses.

Continued and improved emphasis on monitoring also may aid local management decisions, particularly with respect to the effects of livestock grazing. Rangeland science experts identified ground cover as a high monitoring priority for assessing range condition and emphasized the importance of tracking livestock numbers and grazing dates. Ground cover is one of a handful of key variables currently emphasized in BLM monitoring programs, and individual offices are required to collect and report livestock information (numbers, dates). However, the frequency and regularity with which monitoring and livestock data were collected varied considerably across allotments and field offices. The most effective monitoring program may entail both increased data collection effort and the integration of alternative monitoring approaches (for example, remote sensing or monitoring teams).

We also identified three (non-monitoring) datasets that could potentially be used for range-wide analyses. First, BLM maintains spatial (GIS) allotment boundary data. We compiled and corrected the most up-to-date data for use in our analyses. Future efforts would be more streamlined if updated spatial data were maintained in a central location (whereas during our study, we had to obtain data from individual State and Field Offices). Second, at the time of our study, BLM had conducted LHS assessments for 57 percent of all allotments across the west (or for which we had data). After the data had been compiled we mapped land health status across our study region. Third, the BLM maintains allotment-level records of billed and permitted use. We found Billed Use to be a satisfactory indicator of actual timing and intensity of livestock grazing, while permitted use describes the legal maximums. Overall, the BLM may be able to build upon and make refinements to these datasets (for example, rectify cases where an allotment appeared in the spatial boundary dataset, but not the Rangeland Administration System (http://www.blm.gov/ras/), or vice versa; in such cases, we excluded the allotment from our analyses). For all three datasets, the use of allotment boundaries as a basis for geospatial analysis is not without limitations. The allotment boundary is often inclusive of areas not subject to grazing, multiple permittees can operate within an allotment, and often an entire allotment may fail to meet LHS due to factors occurring over a small portion of the allotment.

It nonetheless may be possible to use these spatial datasets to help prioritize monitoring activities over the extensive land areas managed by BLM. For example, we used spatial allotment boundary data and LHS data to test whether remotely sensed vegetation characteristics (see Homer and others, 2008) could be used to predict which allotments met or did not meet LHS. Preliminary results (pending further model validation) suggest that we may be able to use this approach to create risk maps to help BLM prioritize monitoring efforts.

Acknowledgments

Thank you to Sherm Karl, Phil Cooley, Bill Andersen, Craig MacKinnon, Bob Hopper, John Sadowski, Tim Carrigan, John Reitsma, Mike Pellant, Pat Clark, Steve Smith, Steve Knick, Kenneth Visser, and Zack Bowen for their insights and advice, and to additional State and District BLM staff who provided their cooperation and assistance. Thank you to Chris Campton for assistance with field office data collection. We thank Collin Homer, Deb Meyer, and Mike O'Donnell from the USGS for assistance with derived sagebrush map products. We also thank the university and federal range scientists whose insights helped us develop and refine many of the ideas we have presented here; throughout the paper, we have tried to identify concepts that we attribute largely to their input. This research was funded as a part of USGS *Sagebrush Ecosystems Coordinated Research (SECR)*.

References Cited

Adler, P.B., Raff, D.A., and Lauenroth, W.K., 2001, The effect of grazing on the spatial heterogeneity of vegetation: Oecologia, v. 128, no. 4, p. 465-479.

Aldridge, C.L., and Boyce, M.S., 2007, Linking occurrence and fitness to persistence: Habitat-based approach for endangered Greater Sage-Grouse: Ecological Applications, v. 17, no. 2, p. 508-526.

Aldridge, C.L., Nielsen, S.E., Beyer, H.L., Boyce, M.S., Connelly, J.W., Knick, S.T., and Schroeder, M.A., 2008, Range-wide patterns of greater sage-grouse persistence: Diversity and Distributions, v. 14, no. 6, p. 983-994.

Anderson, J.E., and Inouye, R.S., 2001, Landscape-scale changes in plant species abundance and biodiversity of a sagebrush steppe over 45 years: Ecological Monographs, v. 71, no. 4, p. 531-556.

Bestelmeyer, B.T., 2006, Threshold concepts and their use in rangeland management and restoration: The good, the bad, and the insidious: Restoration Ecology, v. 14, no. 3, p. 325-329.

Bestelmeyer, B.T., Tugel, A.J., Peacock, G.L., Robinett, D.G., Sbaver, P.L., Brown, J.R., Herrick, J.E., Sanchez, H., and Havstad, K.M., 2009, State-and-Transition Models for Heterogeneous Landscapes: A Strategy for Development and Application: Rangeland Ecology & Management, v. 62, no. 1, p. 1-15.

Bi-State Local Planning Group. 2004, Greater Sage-Grouse conservation plant for the bi-state plan area of Nevada and eastern California, First Edition.

Booth, D.T., and Cox, S.E., 2008, Image-based monitoring to measure ecological change in rangeland: Frontiers in Ecology and the Environment, v. 6, no. 4, p. 185-190.

Briske, D.D., Derner, J.D., Brown, J.R., Fuhlendorf, S.D., Teague, W.R., Havstad, K.M., Gillen, R.L., Ash, A.J., and Willms, W.D., 2008, Rotational grazing on rangelands: Reconciliation of perception and experimental evidence: Rangeland Ecology & Management, v. 61, no. 1, p. 3-17.

Briske, D.D., and Richards, J.H., 1995, Plant responses to defoliation: a physiological, morphological, and demographic evaluation, *in* Bedunah, D.J., and Sosebee, R.E., eds., Wildland plants: physiological ecology and developmental morphology: Denver, CO, Society for Range Management, p. 635-710.

Bureau of Land Management, 1999, Interagency Technical Reference 1734-4, Bureau of Land Management National Applied Resources Sciences Center.

Bureau of Land Management, 2001, Rangeland Health Standards Handbook H-4180-1. BLM Manual Rel. 4-107.

Burnham, K.P., and Anderson, D.R., 2002, Model selection and multimodel inference: a practical information-theoretic approach. Second edition.: New York, USA, Springer-Verlag, Inc.

Chambers, J.C., and Wisdom, M.J., 2009, Priority Research and Management Issues for the Imperiled Great Basin of the Western United States: Restoration Ecology, v. 17, no. 5, p. 707-714.

Connelly, J.W., Knick, S.T., Schroeder, M.A., and Stiver, S.J., 2004, Conservation assessment of Greater Sage-grouse and sagebrush habitats: Western Association of Fish and Wildlife Agencies. Unpublished report. Cheyenne, WY.

Crawford, J.A., Olson, R.A., West, N.E., Mosley, J.C., Schroeder, M.A., Whitson, T.D., Miller, R.F., Gregg, M.A., and Boyd, C.S., 2004, Ecology and management of sage-grouse and sage-grouse habitat: Journal of Range Management, v. 57, no. 1, p. 2-19.

Dyksterhuis, E.J., 1949, Condition and management of range land based on quantitative ecology: Journal of Range Management v. 2, p. 104-115.

Elzinga, C.L., Salzer, D.W., and Willoughby, J.W., 2001a, Measuring and monitoring plant populations, BLM Technical Reference 1730-1.

Elzinga, C.L., Salzer, D.W., Willoughby, J.W., and Gibbs, J.P., 2001b, Monitoring plant and animal populations: Malden, Massachusetts, Blackwell Science, Inc.

Federal Register 2010, Department of the Interior, Fish and Wildlife Service 50CFR Part17, Endangered and threatened wildlife and plants; 12-month findings for petitions to list the greater sage-grouse (*Centocercus urophasianus*) as threatened or endangered, v. 75, no. 55, p. 13910-14014.

Fedy, B.C., and Aldridge, C.L., 2011, The importance of within-year repeated counts and the influence of scale on long-term monitoring of sage-grouse: Journal of Wildlife Management, vol. 75, no.5, p. 1022-1033.

Fielding, A. H., and Bell, J.F. 1997. A review of methods for the assessment of prediction errors in conservation presence/absence models: Environmental Conservation, v. 24, p. 38–49.

Herrick, J.E., van Zee, J.W., Havstad, K.M., Burkett, L.M., and Whitford, W.G., 2005, Monitoring Manual for Grassland, Shrubland and Savanna Ecosystems, Vol. II: Las Cruces, New Mexico, Jornada Experimental Range.

Herrick, J.E., van Zee, J.W., Havstad, K.M., Burkett, L.M., and Whitford, W.G., 2009, Monitoring Manual for Grassland, Shrubland and Savanna Ecosystems, Vol I.: Las Cruces, New Mexico, Jornada Experimental Range.

Herrick, J.E., van Zee, J.W., Havstad, K.M., and Whitford, W.G., 2001, Monitoring Manual for Grassland, Shrubland and Savanna Ecosystems: Las Cruces, New Mexico, Jornada Experimental Range.

Homer, C.G., Aldridge, C.L., Meyer, D.K., Coan, M.J., and Bowen, Z.H., 2008, Multiscale Sagebrush Rangeland Habitat Modeling in Southwest Wyoming. U.S. Geological Survey Open-File Report 2008-1027.

Homer, C.G., Aldridge, C.L., Meyer, D.K., and Schell, S., *in press*, Multi-scale remote sensing sagebrush characterization with regression trees over Wyoming, USA; laying a foundation for monitoring: Applied Earth Observation and Geoinformation: International Journal of Applied Earth Observation and Geoinformation

Hosmer, D.W., and Lemeshow, S., 2000, Applied logistic regression: New York, New York, USA, John Wiley and Sons, Inc.

Jasmer, G.E., and Holechek, J.L., 1984, Determining Grazing Intensity on Rangeland: Journal of Soil and Water Conservation, v. 39, no. 1, p. 32-35.

Johnson, A.E., James, L.F., and Spillet, J., 1976, The abortifacient and toxic effects of big sagebrush (Artemisia tridentata) and juniper (Juniperus osteosperma) on domestic sheep: Journal of Range Management, v. 29, p. 278-280

Liu, C., Berry, P.M., Dawson, T.P., and Pearson, R.G., 2005, Selecting thresholds of occurrence in the prediction of species distribution: Ecography, v. 28, p. 385-393.

Manel, S., Williams, H.C., and Ormerod, S.J., 2001, Evaluating presence-absence models in ecology: the need to account for prevalence: Journal of Applied Ecology, v. 38, no. 5, p. 921-931.

Miller, R.F., Knick, S.T., Pyke, D.A., Meinke, C.W., Hanser, S.E., Wisdom, M.J., and A.L., H., 2011, Ch. 11: Characteristics of sagebrush habitats and limitations to long-term conservation, Studies in Avian Biology, Ecology and conservation of greater sage-grouse: a landscape species and its habitats: Universit of California Press.

Nichols, M.H., Ruyle, G.B., and Nourbakhsh, I.R., 2009, Very-High-Resolution Panoramic Photography to Improve Conventional Rangeland Monitoring: Rangeland Ecology & Management, v. 62, no. 6, p. 579-582.

Nielsen, S.E., Munro, R.H.M., Bainbridge, E.L., Stenhouse, G.B., and Boyce, M.S., 2004, Grizzly bears and forestry II. Distribution of grizzly bear foods in clearcuts of west-central Alberta, Canada: Forest Ecology and Management, v. 199, no. 1, p. 67-82.

Northern Eagle/Southern Routt Work Group. 2004, Greater Sage-Grouse Conservation Plan for Northern Eagle County and Southern Routt County, Colorado.

Pellant, M., Shaver, P., Pyke, D.A., and Herrick, J.E., 2005, Interpreting Indicators of Rangeland Health-Version 4: Bureau of Land Management, National Science and Technology Center Technical Reference 1734-6.

Pyke, D.A., Herrick, J.E., Shaver, P., and Pellant, M., 2002, Rangeland health attributes and indicators for qualitative assessment: Journal of Range Management, v. 55, p. 584-597.

Rango, A., Laliberte, A., Herrick, J.E., Winters, C., Havstad, K., Steele, C., and Browning, D., 2009, Unmanned aerial vehicle-based remote sensing for rangeland assessment, monitoring, and management: Journal of Applied Remote Sensing, v. 3, p. 1-15.

Schroeder, M.A., Aldridge, C.L., Apa, A.D., Bohne, J.R., Braun, C.E., Bunnell, S.D., Connelly, J.W., Deibert, P.A., Gardner, S.C., Hilliard, M.A., Kobriger, G.D., McAdam, S.M., McCarthy, C.W., McCarthy, J.J., Mitchell, D.L., Rickerson, E.V., and Stiver, S.J., 2004, Distribution of sage-grouse in North America: Condor, v. 106, no. 2, p. 363-376.

Smith, S.D., Bunting, S.C., and Hironaka, M., 1986, Sensitivity of Frequency Plots for Detecting Vegetation Change: Northwest Science, v. 60, no. 4, p. 279-286.

Stoddart, L.A., Smith, A.D., and Box, T.W., 1995, Range management, 3rd edition: New York, NY, McGraw-Hill.

Swets, J.A., 1988, Measuring the Accuracy of Diagnostic Systems: Science, v. 240, no. 4857, p. 1285-1293.

Task Group on Unity in Concepts and Terminology Committee Members. 1995, New concepts for assessment of rangeland condition: Journal of Range Management, v. 48, p. 271-282.

Thurow, T.L., and Taylor, C.A., 1999, Viewpoint: The role of drought in range management: Journal of Range Management, v. 52, no. 5, p. 413-419.

Tongway, D.J., 1994, Rangeland soil condition assessment manual, CSIRO Publication, Melbourne, p. 1-16.

U.S. Department of Agriculture, Natural Resources Conservation Service, 2006, Chapter 4: Inventorying and monitoring grazing land resources, National range and pasture handbook.

U.S. Department of Agriculture, Natural Resources Conservation Service, 2009a, Chapter 3: Ecological sites and forage suitability groups, National range and pasture handbook, accessed January 3, 2011, at *http://www.glti.nrcs.usda.gov/technical/publications/nrph.html.*

U.S. Department of Agriculture, Natural Resources Conservation Service, 2009b, Chapter 4: Inventorying and monitoring grazing land resources, National range and pasture handbook, accessed January 3, 2011, at *http://www.glti.nrcs.usda.gov/technical/publications/nrph.html.*

U.S. Department of Agriculture, Natural Resources Conservation Service, 2009c, National range and pasture handbook, accessed January 3, 2011, at *http://www.glti.nrcs.usda.gov/technical/publications/nrph.html.*

Vallentine, J.F., 1990, Grazing Management: San Diego, CA, Academic Press, Inc.

West, N.E., 2003, History of rangeland monitoring in the USA: Arid Land Research & Management, v. 17, p. 495-545.

Westoby, M., Walker, B., and Noy-Meir, I., 1989, Opportunistic management for rangelands not at equilibrium: Journal of Range Management, v. 42, no. 4, p. 266-274.

Williams, B.K., Szaro, R.C., and Shapiro, C.D., 2007, Adaptive management: the U.S. Department of the Interior technical guide: Washington, D.C., U.S. Department of the Interior, Adaptive Management Working Group.

Xian, G., Homer, C.G., and Aldridge, C.L., *in press*, Assessing Long-Term Variations of Sagebrush Habitat – Characterization of Spatial Extents and Distribution Patterns Using Multi-temporal Satellite Remote Sensing Data: International Journal of Remote Sensing.

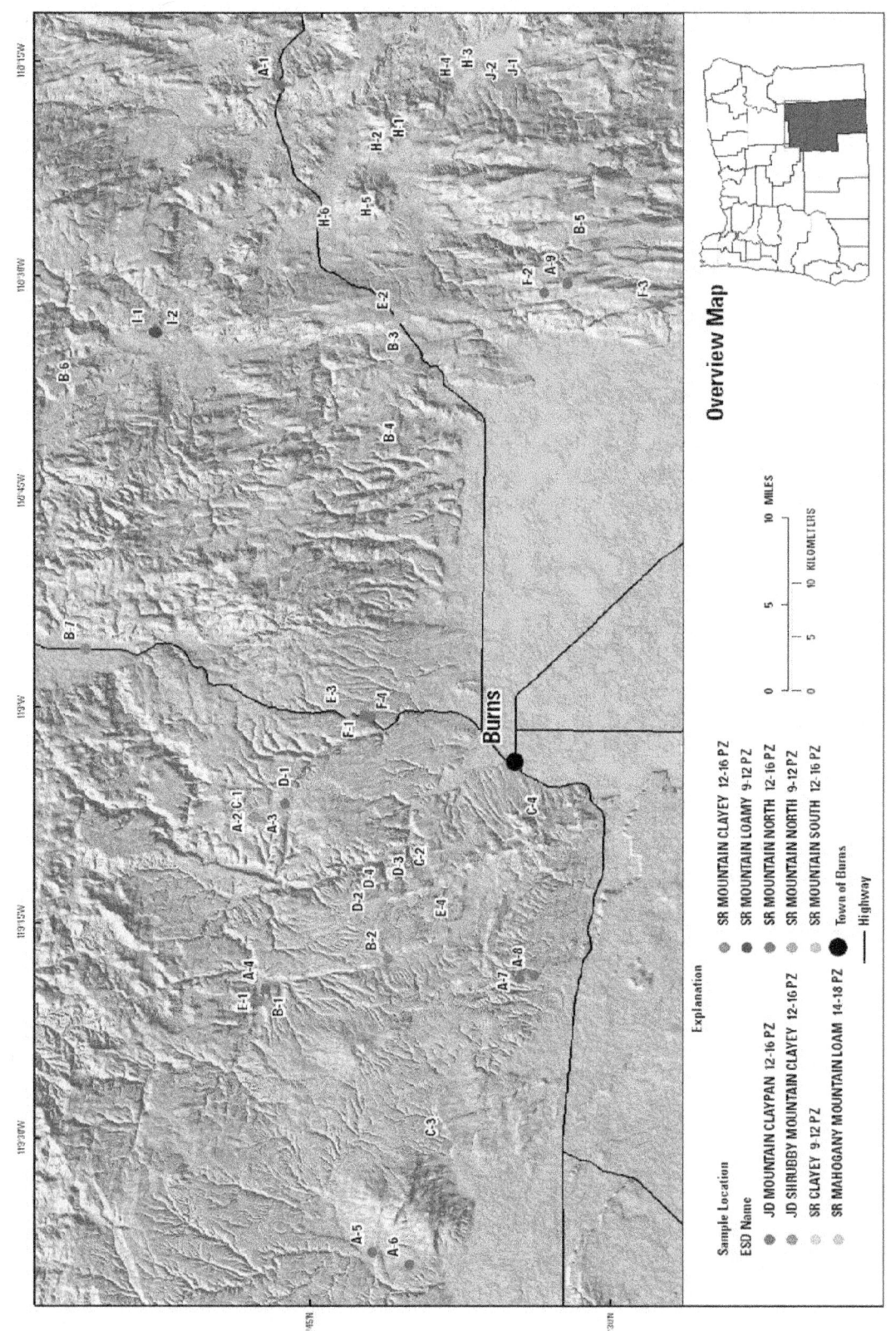

Figure 1. Sample sites in Harney County, Oregon where production was estimated with NRCS reconstruction methods.

34

Production: predicted ranges and field estimates

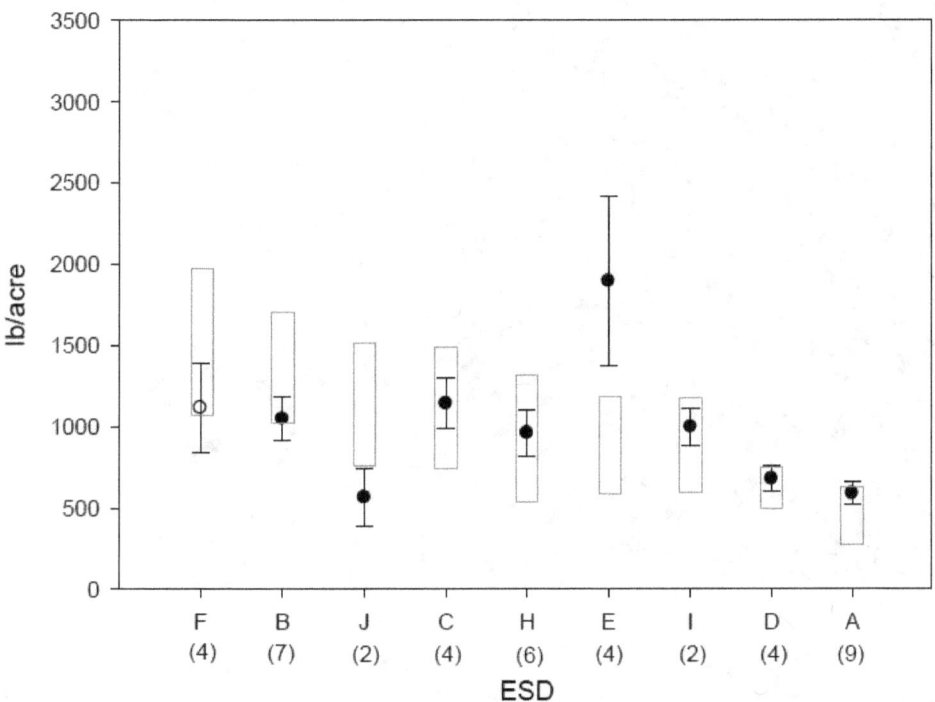

Figure 2. Predicted ranges and field estimates of production. Filled-circles are field data samples of production ±1SE (estimated using NRCS reconstruction methods), and boxes indicates the predicted range of production values according to Ecological Site Descriptions (ESD). A= JD Mountain Claypan 12-16PZ, B=SR Mountain Clayey 12-16 PZ, C=JD Shrubby Mountain Clayey 12-16PZ, D=SR Mahogany Mountain Loam 14-18PZ, E=SR Mountain South 12-16PZ, F=SR Mountain North 12-16PZ, H= SR Clayey 9-12PZ, I=SR Mountain Loamy 9-12 PZ, J=SR Mountain North 9-12PZ. Parentheses indicate sample sizes.

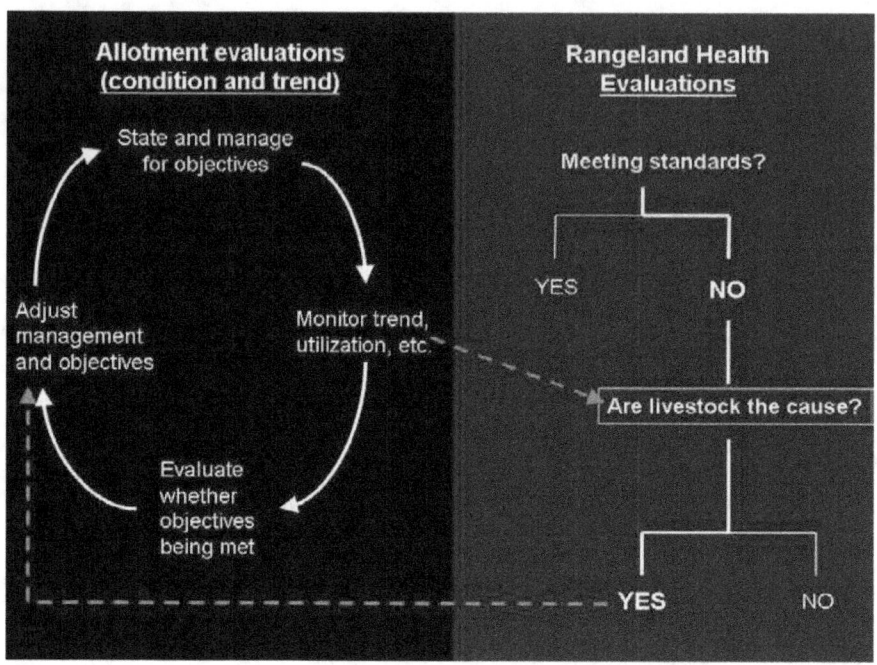

Figure 3. Schematic of (1) the BLM allotment evaluation process which is based on quantitative monitoring data and (2) the Land Health Standards (LHS) Evaluation process which is based on rangeland health indicators. Red arrows indicate feedbacks between the two processes.

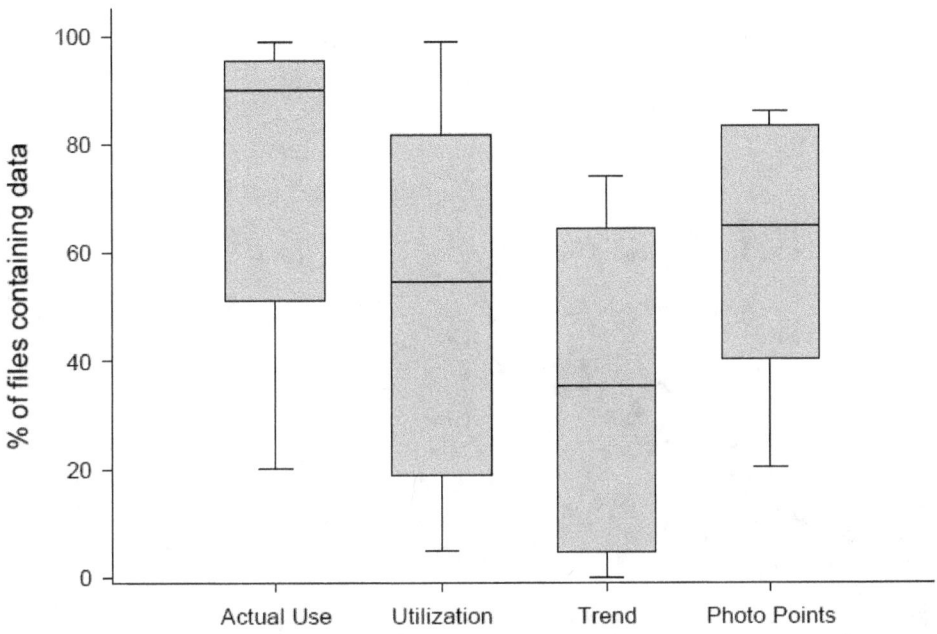

Figure 4. Box plot showing percentage of BLM files containing Actual Use, Utilization, Trend and Photo Point data. Plots indicate median, 25/75 percentile, and 10/90 percentile for 13 field offices. ANOVA results indicate data availability differed significantly among the four data types ($F_{3,36}$=7.56, p=.0005)

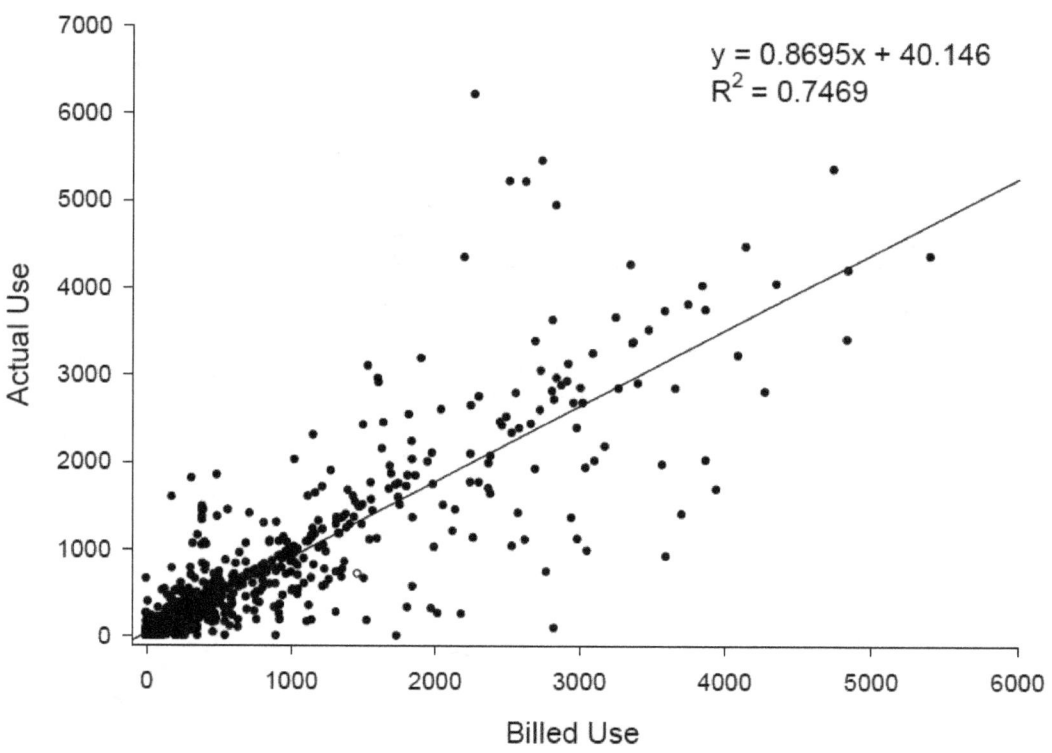

Figure 5. Relationship between yearly AUMs billed (Billed Use) by the Bureau of Land Management and AUMs (Actual Use) reported by permittees on 171 BLM allotments. Data points (n=906) represent allotment-year combinations between 1998 and 2007. Data points (n=42) from ten allotments that permit ≥ 5000 AUMs/year (n=42) were excluded due to under-reporting associated with large allotments used by multiple permittees.

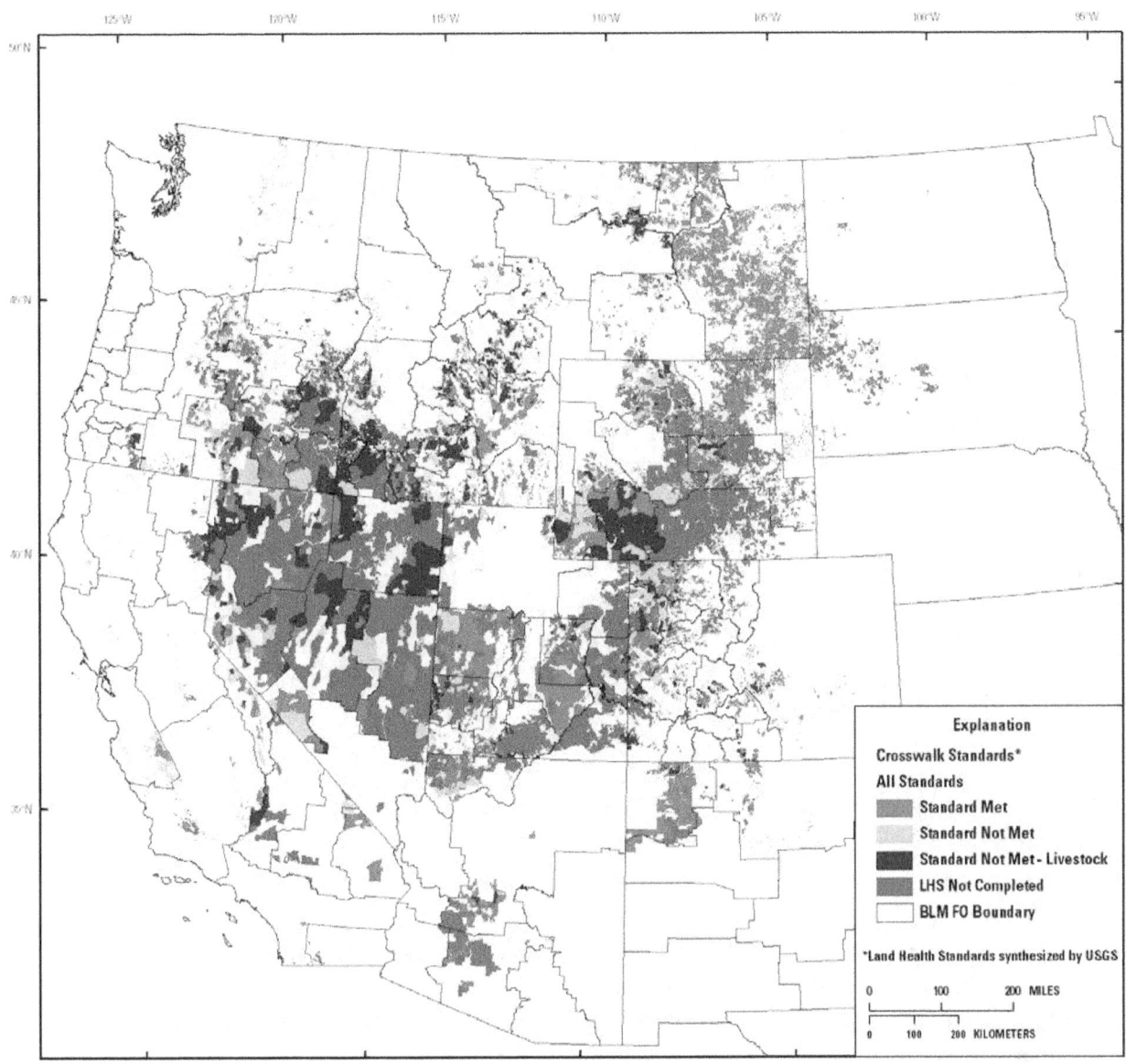

Figure 6. Spatial representation of whether BLM allotments have met Land Health Standards (LHS) (Upland, Riparian and Biodiversity) and whether livestock have contributed to unmet LHS. Data provided by BLM.

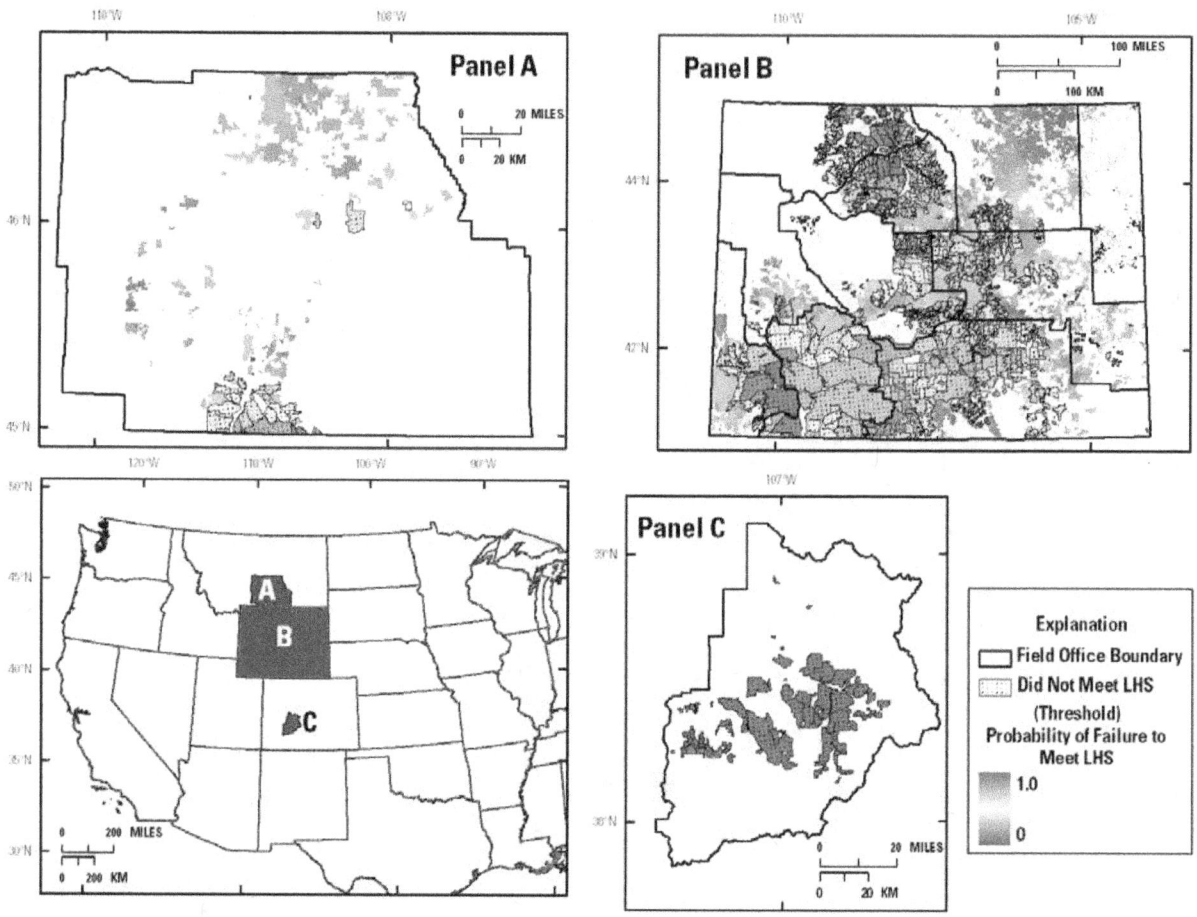

Figure 7. Predicted probability (risk) of any given BLM allotment not meeting Land Health Standards (LHS) across Montana (Billings BLM Field Office, Panel A), Wyoming (State-wide, Panel B), and Colorado (Gunnison Basin, Panel C). The model was developed using available data for 1,131 LHS assessments in the region, for which 798 met LHS and 333 did not meet LHS. A total of 1,510 of 3,564 allotments are at risk of not meeting LHS (crosshatching), based on an optimal model probability classification point of 0.271.

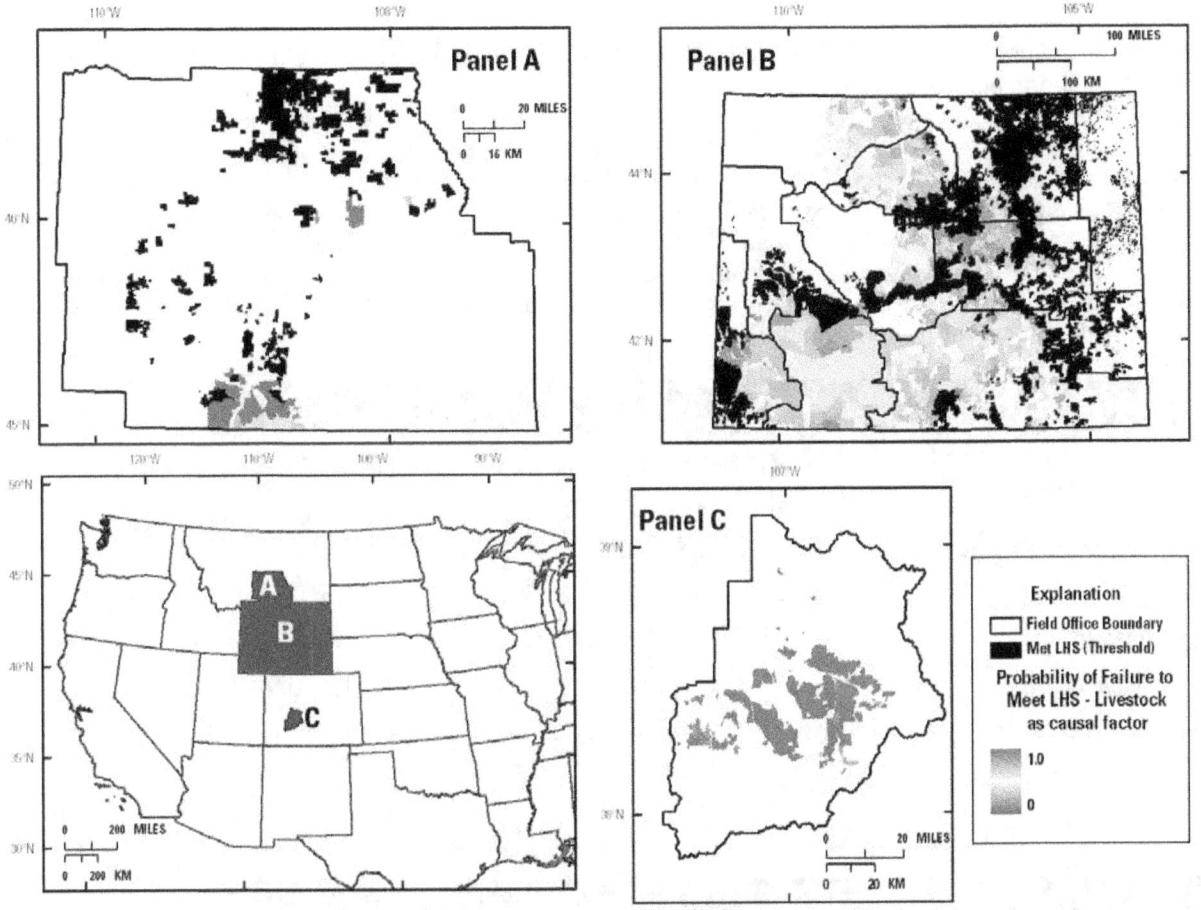

Figure 8. Predicted probability (risk) of not meeting standards, with livestock being the primary cause. Predictions are shown for all BLM allotments not meeting Land Health Standards (LHS) across Montana (Billings BLM Field Office, Panel A), Wyoming (State-wide, Panel B), and Colorado (Gunnison Basin, Panel C). A total of 1,131 LHS assessments in the region, for which 798 met LHS and 333 did not meet LHS.

Table 1. Top table summarizes office file results from 310 allotments selected at random across 13 Bureau of Land Management (BLM) field offices.

[Bottom table summarizes results from 62 of 310 allotments that cited livestock grazing as reason for not meeting at least one Land Health Standard. In both tables, allotments are divided into those being managed to "Maintain" vs. "Improve" rangeland condition. For each data type, "Freq." indicates the percentage of allotments across the region with at least 1 year of data between 1997 and 2007 (although completeness of data within a given allotment is variable, for example, some allotments may have data for only a subset of key areas or pastures). The "mean # years" column indicates the average number of years for which data exist ± 1 SE (excluding allotments that had no data). AMP = Allotment Management Plan]

ALL SAMPLED ALLOTMENTS				
Data type	**Maintain (n=109)**		**Improve (n=201)**	
	Freq.	**mean # yrs**	**Freq.**	**mean # yrs**
1) Actual Use	59%	6.3±0.46	77%	6.8±0.29
2) Utilization	51%	4.4±0.47	52%	4.7±0.33
3) Vegetation Trend	34%	1.0±0	38%	1.04±0.03
4) Photo Points	53%	1.3±0.06	61%	1.7± 0.09
AMP or Grazing Plan	17%	-.-	26%	-.-
Allotment Evaluation	15%	-.-	8%	-.-

ALLOTMENTS CITING LIVESTOCK ISSUES				
Data type	**Maintain (n=17)**		**Improve (n=45)**	
	Freq.	**mean # yrs**	**Freq.**	**mean # yrs**
1) Actual Use	47%	5±1.22	84%	3.66±0.59
2) Utilization	53%	2.56±1.07	51%	4.43±0.69
3) Vegetation Trend	35%	1.0±0	36%	1.01±0.03
4) Photo Points	65%	1.6±0.19	71%	2.02±0.22
All 4 data types	35%	-.-	24%	-.-
Data types 1,2,3	35%	-.-	27%	-.-
Data types 1, 2	42%	-.-	49%	-.-
No data	29%	-.-	9%	-.-

Table 2. Types of data (collected between 1997 and 2007) contained in a randomly selected sample of 310 allotment files from 13 Bureau of Land Management (BLM) offices across 6 States.

[All Frequency, Cover, and Production techniques are described in the 1996 Interagency Technical Reference 1734-4, except Line-point, which is a variation of the point-intercept method. All Utilization techniques are described in the 1996 Interagency Technical Reference 1734-3, except the Utilization Gauge method which is a US Forest Service stubble height method. Both "State D" offices also collected Observed Apparent Trend data, a subjective numerical rating that considers vigor, seedlings, surface litter, pedestals and gullies. Offices A-1, C-1, D-1 and D-2 also used 3 × 3 feet or 5 × 5 feet Range Trend Plots for visual estimates of key species attributes such as cover, frequency, density, and vigor; specific methodology varied across BLM offices]

Office	Frequency (and ground cover)			Cover					Production (and composition)		Utilization				Photo points
	quadrat freq.	nested freq.	pace freq.	Daub-enmire	Line intercept	Line-point	Step point	Method not specified	Dry-weight-rank	Com-parative yield	Grazed-class	Height-weight	Util-ization gauge	Key species	
A-1	X		X					X	X		X			X	X
B-1	X			X										X	X
B-2														X	X
C-1	X							X						X	X
C-2	X				X	X				X				X	X
D-1							X							X	X
D-2		X		X	X		X							X	X
E-1	X	X		X	X									X	X
E-2												X		X	X
F-1														X	X
F-2								X						X	X
F-3								X					X	X	X
F-4					X		X								X

43

Table 3. Results of Land Health Standards (LHS) evaluations conducted by Bureau of Land Management (BLM) allotments between 1997 and 2007.

[Allotments are divided into those managed to "Maintain" vs. "Improve" rangeland condition. For allotments that had "Not met" a standard, the "Livestock-caused" column indicates the percentage of "Not met" due to livestock. Top table summarizes whether allotments met all of their state standards (three to eight, depending on state). Other tables summarize three standards common to all states (Upland Soil, Riparian, and Biodiversity). ANOVA indicates significant differences in meeting of "all standards" between Maintain and Improve allotments ($F_{1,18}=7.74$, p=0.02) and across states ($F_{9,18}=31.27$, p=<0.0001). Standards that were "Not met" due to livestock differed significantly across states ($F_{9,18}=3.14$, p=0.02) and among Upland, Riparian and Biodiversity standards ($F_{2,18}=5.18$, p=0.02), and there was a significant interaction between standards (Upland, Riparian, Biodiversity) and allotment status (Maintain, Improve) ($F_{2,18}==21.09$, p<0.0001). Raw LHS data supplied by BLM]

	ALL STANDARDS							
	"MAINTAIN" ALLOTMENTS			"IMPROVE" ALLOTMENTS			NO DATA	
State	All stds met	≥1 std Not met	Livestock-caused	All stds met	≥1 std Not met	Livestock-caused		
A	n=67 73%	27%	11%	n=83 66%	34%	14%	n=189	56%
B	n=182 71%	29%	42%	n=461 64%	36%	47%	n=292	31%
C	n=62 35%	65%	55%	n=57 25%	75%	72%	n=409	77%
D	n=204 61%	39%	56%	n=262 52%	48%	46%	n=353	43%
E	n=140 79%	21%	52%	n=246 82%	18%	43%	n=565	59%
F	n=385 70%	30%	23%	n=352 47%	53%	30%	n=862	54%
G	n=100 63%	37%	14%	n=107 34%	66%	34%	n=71	26%
H	n=371 63%	37%	45%	n=469 39%	61%	60%	n=583	41%
I	n=1463 87%	13%	47%	n=670 68%	32%	56%	n=124	5%
J	n=130 89%	11%	14%	n=180 85%	15%	41%	n=1093	78%
TOTAL	n=3104 77%	23%	41%	n=2887 59%	41%	48%	n=4541	43%

44

Table 3. Results of Land Health Standards (LHS) evaluations conducted by Bureau of Land Management (BLM) allotments between 1997 and 2007.—Continued.

[Allotments are divided into those managed to "Maintain" vs. "Improve" rangeland condition. For allotments that had "Not met" a standard, the "Livestock-caused" column indicates the percentage of "Not met" due to livestock. Top table summarizes whether allotments met all of their state standards (three to eight, depending on state). Other tables summarize three standards common to all states (Upland Soil, Riparian, and Biodiversity). ANOVA indicates significant differences in meeting of "all standards" between Maintain and Improve allotments ($F_{1,18}$=7.74, p=0.02) and across states ($F_{9,18}$=31.27, p=<0.0001). Standards that were "Not met" due to livestock differed significantly across states ($F_{9,18}$=3.14, p=0.02) and among Upland, Riparian and Biodiversity standards ($F_{2,18}$=5.18, p=0.02), and there was a significant interaction between standards (Upland, Riparian, Biodiversity) and allotment status (Maintain, Improve) ($F_{2,18}$= 21.09, p<.0001). Raw LHS data supplied by BLM]

| | UPLAND SOIL STANDARD | | | | | | |
| | "MAINTAIN" ALLOTMENTS | | | "IMPROVE" ALLOTMENTS | | | NO DATA |
State	Met	Not met	Livestock-caused	Met	Not met	Livestock-caused	
A	96%	4%	0% n=54	96%	4%	0% n=67	64% n=218
B	87%	13%	39% n=182	79%	21%	48% n=457	32% n=296
C	81%	19%	73% n=57	60%	40%	68% n=55	79% n=416
D	87%	13%	50% n=204	85%	15%	35% n=260	43% n=355
E	95%	5%	71% n=140	91%	9%	43% n=246	59% n=565
F	91%	9%	34% n=375	85%	15%	31% n=336	56% n=888
G	98%	2%	50% n=96	93%	7%	50% n=88	34% n=94
H	95%	5%	71% n=371	79%	21%	67% n=464	41% n=588
I	95%	5%	57% n=1455	93%	7%	73% n=656	6% n=146
J	93%	7%	0% n=127	87%	13%	48% n=178	78% n=1098
TOTAL	93%	7%	50% n=3061	86%	14%	53% n=2807	44% n=4664

Table 3. Results of Land Health Standards (LHS) evaluations conducted by Bureau of Land Management (BLM) allotments between 1997 and 2007—Continued.

[Allotments are divided into those managed to "Maintain" vs. "Improve" rangeland condition. For allotments that had "Not met" a standard, the "Livestock-caused" column indicates the percentage of "Not met" due to livestock. Top table summarizes whether allotments met all of their state standards (three to eight, depending on state). Other tables summarize three standards common to all states (Upland Soil, Riparian, and Biodiversity). ANOVA indicates significant differences in meeting of "all standards" between Maintain and Improve allotments ($F_{1,18}$=7.74, p=0.02) and across states ($F_{9,18}$=31.27, p=<0.0001). Standards that were "Not met" due to livestock differed significantly across states ($F_{9,18}$=3.14, p=0.02) and among Upland, Riparian and Biodiversity standards ($F_{2,18}$=5.18, p=0.02), and there was a significant interaction between standards (Upland, Riparian, Biodiversity) and allotment status (Maintain, Improve) ($F_{2,18}$== 21.09, p<.0001). Raw LHS data supplied by BLM]

RIPARIAN STANDARD

State	"MAINTAIN" ALLOTMENTS				"IMPROVE" ALLOTMENTS				NO DATA	
		Met	Not met	Livestock-caused		Met	Not met	Livestock-caused		
A	n=54	94%	6%	33%	n=67	96%	4%	67%	n=218	64%
B	n=182	94%	6%	73%	n=457	88%	12%	72%	n=296	32%
C	n=56	70%	30%	65%	n=47	36%	64%	83%	n=362	78%
D	n=200	75%	25%	66%	n=260	66%	34%	49%	n=359	44%
E	n=139	91%	9%	77%	n=246	93%	7%	82%	n=566	60%
F	n=371	86%	14%	40%	n=324	75%	25%	49%	n=904	57%
G	n=96	89%	11%	9%	n=87	70%	30%	77%	n=95	34%
H	n=358	85%	15%	68%	n=436	66%	34%	72%	n=629	44%
I	n=1459	93%	7%	61%	n=656	77%	23%	68%	n=142	6%
J	n=130	100%	0%	0%	n=180	98%	2%	100%	n=1093	78%
TOTAL	n=3045	90%	10%	59%	n=2760	78%	22%	66%	n=4664	45%

Table 3. Results of Land Health Standards (LHS) evaluations conducted by Bureau of Land Management (BLM) allotments between 1997 and 2007.—Continued

[Allotments are divided into those managed to "Maintain" vs. "Improve" rangeland condition. For allotments that had "Not met" a standard, the "Livestock-caused" column indicates the percentage of "Not met" due to livestock. Top table summarizes whether allotments met all of their state standards (three to eight, depending on state). Other tables summarize three standards common to all states (Upland Soil, Riparian, and Biodiversity). ANOVA indicates significant differences in meeting of "all standards" between Maintain and Improve allotments ($F_{1,18}=7.74$, p=0.02) and across states ($F_{9,18}=31.27$, p=<0.0001). Standards that were "Not met" due to livestock differed significantly across states ($F_{9,18}=3.14$, p=0.02) and among Upland, Riparian and Biodiversity standards ($F_{2,18}=5.18$, p=0.02), and there was a significant interaction between standards (Upland, Riparian, Biodiversity) and allotment status (Maintain, Improve) ($F_{2,18}= 21.09$, p<.0001). Raw LHS data supplied by BLM]

	BIODIVERSITY STANDARD								
	"MAINTAIN" ALLOTMENTS				"IMPROVE" ALLOTMENTS				NO DATA
State		Met	Not met	Livestock-caused		Met	Not met	Livestock-caused	
A	n=68	84%	16%	36%	n=55	93%	7%	25%	n=216 64%
B	n=459	74%	26%	50%	n=182	75%	25%	40%	n=294 31%
C	n=55	40%	60%	67%	n=59	51%	49%	52%	n=414 78%
D	n=260	65%	35%	40%	n=204	74%	26%	50%	n=355 43%
E	n=245	87%	13%	31%	n=140	86%	14%	45%	n=566 60%
F	n=341	77%	23%	33%	n=375	88%	12%	30%	n=883 55%
G	n=88	72%	28%	36%	n=96	79%	21%	20%	n=94 34%
H	n=466	54%	46%	61%	n=367	74%	26%	43%	n=590 41%
I	n=665	88%	12%	58%	n=1460	94%	6%	32%	n=132 6%
J	n=178	87%	13%	43%	n=128	91%	9%	18%	n=1097 78%
TOTAL	n=2825	75%	25%	50%	n=3066	87%	13%	39%	n=4641 44%

47

Table 4. Results of informal conversations with federal and university rangeland science experts on how best to prioritize monitoring of rangeland condition and livestock impacts.

[Experts were presented with a hypothetical monitoring scenario (appendix 5). Although we spoke with 22 university scientists, three participated in a group conversation and expressed consensus opinions; they are therefore counted as a single expert]

Monitoring priority	Federal (n=20)	University (n=20)
cover	55%	70%
bare ground	25%	15%
gap	5%	5%
production	10%	10%
frequency	5%	0%
density	10%	10%
utilization	35%	25%
cattle and/or wildlife condition	5%	10%
soils	25%	10%
reference areas or ecological sites	30%	40%
photos	30%	15%
remote sensing	30%	35%
identification of at-risk areas	25%	15%

Additional insights:		
Perceived disincentive to report under-grazing	5%	0%
Photo points compelling in court	5%	0%
Effectiveness of monitoring teams	0%	5%

Table 5. Mean, standard deviation (Std) and t-test comparisons of sagebrush vegetation characteristics for allotments in Montana (Billings BLM Field Office), Wyoming (State-wide), and Colorado (Gunnison Basin) that have "Met" (798) versus "Not met" (333) Land Health Standards (LHS) assessments.

[Cover variables include sagebrush (sb), herbaceous (hb), litter (lt), and bare (ba); metrics assessed include mean, median and standard deviation (std)]

Variable/metric	Met		Not Met		t-test means comparison		
	Mean	Std	Mean	Std	t-value	df	p-value
sb_mean	9.882	4.060	8.167	4.073	6.460	619.971	0.0000
sb_std	3.520	1.153	3.129	1.313	4.722	555.894	0.0000
sb_median	9.830	4.464	8.117	4.447	5.896	624.049	0.0000
hb_mean	24.320	11.037	18.236	9.881	9.112	689.802	0.0000
hb_std	7.510	3.003	6.778	2.878	3.849	646.623	0.0001
hb_median	23.972	11.533	17.697	10.519	8.885	677.587	0.0000
lt_mean	21.013	6.792	18.233	7.332	5.936	581.274	0.0000
lt_std	6.149	1.871	5.825	1.750	2.779	661.487	0.0056
lt_median	21.060	7.453	18.060	7.976	5.876	585.625	0.0000
ba_mean	42.677	14.128	52.357	16.035	-9.575	557.569	0.0000
ba_std	11.828	3.374	11.426	3.338	1.840	627.959	0.0663
ba_median	41.711	15.429	52.306	17.544	-9.583	556.733	0.0000

Table 6. Mean, standard deviation (Std) and t-test comparisons of sagebrush vegetation characteristics for allotments in Montana (Billings BLM Field Office), Wyoming (State-wide), and Colorado (Gunnison Basin) that did not meet Land Health Standards (LHS) assessments due to livestock (132) versus other causes (201).

[Cover variables include sagebrush (sb), herbaceous (hb), litter (lt), and bare (ba); metrics assessed include mean, median and standard deviation (std)]

Variable/metric	Other causes		Livestock as cause		t-test means comparison		
	Mean	Std	Mean	Std	t-value	df	p-value
sb_mean	7.592	4.029	9.042	3.998	-3.226	281.887	0.0014
sb_std	3.017	1.370	3.300	1.207	-1.982	303.930	0.0484
sb_median	7.557	4.407	8.970	4.388	-2.869	281.211	0.0044
hb_mean	16.988	8.796	20.136	11.104	-2.740	235.078	0.0066
hb_std	6.546	2.429	7.132	3.430	-1.704	216.167	0.0899
hb_median	16.498	9.322	19.523	11.924	-2.462	232.715	0.0145
lt_mean	17.425	7.547	19.465	6.838	-2.554	299.060	0.0111
lt_std	5.604	1.708	6.163	1.767	-2.860	273.593	0.0046
lt_median	17.294	8.166	19.227	7.560	-2.211	295.149	0.0278
ba_mean	54.831	16.069	48.591	5.288	3.570	290.048	0.0004
ba_std	10.990	3.335	12.091	3.244	-2.995	285.738	0.0030
ba_median	54.721	17.506	48.629	17.018	3.159	285.895	0.0018

Table 7. Candidate models for each metric [mean, median and standard deviation (std)] within each variable subgroup comparing sagebrush vegetation characteristics for allotments in Montana (Billings BLM Field Office), Wyoming (State-wide), and Colorado (Gunnison Basin) that have "Met" (798) versus "Not met" (333) Land Health Standards (LHS) assessments.

[See table 5 for a definition of model variables. State is a categorical variable with Wyoming as the indicator. Log likelihood (LL) and number of parameters in the model (K) are shown. Models are ranked by ΔAIC_c within each variable subgroup. In all cases, the top AIC_c selected model was carried forward for candidate model building]

Model	LL	K	AIC_c	ΔAIC_c
Sagebrush				
sb_mean state	-625.632	4	1259.334	0.000
sb_mean sb_std state	-625.492	5	1261.091	1.756
sb_median state	-629.120	4	1266.310	6.976
sb_median sb_std state	-628.609	5	1267.325	7.990
sb_std state	-645.055	4	1298.180	38.846
Litter				
lt_mean state	-636.669	4	1281.41	0.000
lt_median state	-637.550	4	1283.17	1.761
lt_mean lt_std state	-636.652	5	1283.41	2.002
lt_median lt_std state	-637.454	5	1285.02	3.606
lt_std state	-649.426	4	1306.92	25.514
Herbaceous				
hb_mean hb_std state	-616.028	5	1242.16	0.000
hb_median hb_std state	-619.871	5	1249.85	7.685
hb_mean state	-620.943	4	1249.96	7.794
hb_median state	-622.534	4	1253.14	10.975
hb_std state	-649.540	4	1307.15	64.987
Bare				
ba_mean ba_std state	-607.959	5	1226.03	0.000
ba_mean state	-610.153	4	1228.38	2.351
ba_median ba_std state	-609.372	5	1228.85	2.825
ba_median state	-611.533	4	1231.14	5.113
ba_std state	-651.163	4	1310.40	84.372

Table 8. Final candidate models comparing sagebrush vegetation characteristics for allotments in Montana (Billings BLM Field Office), Wyoming (State-wide), and Colorado (Gunnison Basin) that have "Met" (798) versus "Not met" (333) Land Health Standards (LHS) assessments.

[See table 5 for a definition of model variables. State is a categorical variable with Wyoming as the indicator. Log likelihood (LL) and number of parameters in the model (K) are shown. Models are ranked by ΔAIC_c with Akaike weight (w_i) indicating the weight of evidence for each model within the candidate set]

Model	LL	K	AIC$_c$	ΔAIC$_c$	w_i
sb_mean hb_mean hb_std state	-594.716	6	1201.582	0.000	1.000
sb_mean ba_mean ba_std state	-603.873	6	1219.896	18.315	0.000
ba_mean ba_std state	-607.959	5	1226.025	24.444	0.000
lt_mean hb_mean hb_std state	-610.437	6	1233.024	31.443	0.000
hb_mean hb_std state	-616.028	5	1242.164	40.582	0.000
sb_mean state	-625.632	4	1259.334	57.753	0.000
sb_mean lt_mean state	-625.306	5	1260.719	59.138	0.000

Table 9. The coefficients (β) and standard errors (SE) of the variables in the top AIC$_c$-selected models comparing sagebrush vegetation characteristics for allotments in Montana (Billings BLM Field Office), Wyoming (State-wide), and Colorado (Gunnison Basin) that have "Met" (798) versus "Not met" (333) Land Health Standards (LHS) assessments.

[Model variables include sagebrush (sb), herbaceous (hb), and state as categorical variable with Wyoming as the indicator. See Table 5 for a definition of model variables. State is a categorical variable with Wyoming as the indicator; state_1 is Colorado and state_2 is Montana]

Parameter	β	SE
sb_mean	-0.118	0.019
hb_mean	-0.065	0.01
hb_std	0.044	0.034
state_1	3.468	0.746
state_2	-0.146	0.217
constant	1.198	0.283

Table 10. Candidate models for each metric [mean, median and standard deviation (std)] within each variable subgroup comparing sagebrush vegetation characteristics for allotments in Montana (Billings BLM Field Office), Wyoming (State-wide), and Colorado (Gunnison Basin) that did not meet Land Health Standards (LHS) assessments due to livestock (132) versus other causes (201).

[See table 5 for a definition of model variables. State is a categorical variable with Wyoming as the indicator. Log likelihood (LL) and number of parameters in the model (K) are shown. Models are ranked by ΔAIC_c within each variable subgroup. In all cases, the top AIC_c-selected model was carried forward for candidate model building]

Model	LL	K	AIC_c	ΔAIC_c
Sagebrush				
sb_mean state	-209.818	4	427.880	0.000
sb_mean sb_std state	-209.439	5	429.246	1.366
sb_median state	-210.981	4	430.205	2.325
sb_median sb_std state	-210.243	5	430.854	2.974
sb_std state	-212.020	4	432.285	4.405
Litter				
lt_std state	-212.738	4	433.719	0.000
lt_mean lt_std state	-212.245	5	434.857	1.138
lt_mean state	-213.422	4	435.088	1.369
lt_median lt_std state	-212.404	5	435.174	1.455
lt_median state	-213.812	4	435.867	2.148
Herbaceous				
hb_mean state	-213.746	4	435.736	0.000
hb_median state	-214.100	4	436.444	0.708
hb_std state	-214.336	4	436.916	1.180
hb_mean hb_std state	-213.712	5	437.791	2.055
hb_median hb_std state	-213.962	5	438.291	2.555
Bare				
ba_mean ba_std state	-208.917	5	428.200	0.000
ba_median ba_std state	-209.503	5	429.374	1.173
ba_std state	-211.468	4	431.180	2.980
ba_mean state	-212.533	4	433.310	5.110
ba_median state	-213.214	4	434.673	6.473

Table 11. Final candidate models comparing sagebrush vegetation characteristics for allotments in Montana (Billings BLM Field Office), Wyoming (State-wide), and Colorado (Gunnison Basin) that failed to meet Land Health Standards (LHS) due to livestock (132) versus other causes (201).

[See table 5 for a definition of model variables. State is a categorical variable with Wyoming as the indicator. Log likelihood (LL) and number of parameters in the model (K) are shown. Models are ranked by ΔAIC_c with Akaike weight (w_i) indicating the weight of evidence for each model within the candidate set]

Model	LL	K	AIC_c	ΔAIC_c	w_i
sb_mean ba_mean ba_std state	-206.157	6	424.829	0.000	0.416
sb_mean lt_std ba_mean ba_std state	-205.560	7	425.810	0.980	0.255
sb_mean state	-209.818	4	427.880	3.051	0.091
ba_mean ba_std state	-208.917	5	428.200	3.371	0.077
sb_mean hb_mean state	-208.969	5	428.306	3.477	0.073
sb_mean lt_std state	-209.300	5	428.966	4.137	0.053
lt_mean ba_mean ba_std state	-208.897	6	430.310	5.481	0.027
lt_std state	-212.738	4	433.719	8.890	0.005
hb_mean state	-213.746	4	435.736	10.907	0.002
lt_mean hb_mean state	-212.925	5	436.216	11.387	0.001

Table 12. The coefficients (β) and standard errors (SE) of the variables in the top AIC_c –selected models comparing sagebrush vegetation characteristics for allotments in Montana (Billings BLM Field Office), Wyoming (State-wide), and Colorado (Gunnison Basin) that failed to meet Land Health Standards (LHS) assessments due to livestock (132) versus other causes (201).

[Model variables include sagebrush (sb), bare (ba), and litter (lt), and state as categorical variable with Wyoming as the indicator. See table 5 for a definition of model variables. State is a categorical variable with Wyoming as the indicator; state_1 is Colorado and state_2 is Montana]

| Parameter | Top Model | | Second Model | |
	β	SE	β	SE
sb_mean	0.084	0.036	0.099	0.039
ba_mean	-0.005	0.011	-0.006	0.011
ba_std	0.096	0.036	0.132	0.049
lt_mean			-0.109	0.1
state_1	1.154	0.41	1.193	0.413
state_2	0.952	0.44	1.016	0.446
Constant	-2.238	0.913	-2.084	0.926

Appendix 1. Spatial Allotment Data

Introduction

The overall objective of this exercise was to assess the available spatial data for Bureau of Land Management (BLM) grazing allotments and determine if it was feasible to combine spatial data with tabular data to describe important attributes of allotments. The second goal was to join the spatial data with tabular data describing the distribution of Land Health Standards (LHS) assessed on grazing allotments. Finally, we wanted to use the compiled spatial datasets to investigate relationships among livestock grazing, land health status, and sagebrush cover.

Once we determined that use of the existing data would not be feasible, the primary objective was adapted to develop a usable topologically enforced coarse dataset of grazing allotments administered by the BLM. In particular, this exercise sought to limit/eliminate problems associated with gaps, slivers, edge matching issues, duplicate polygons and attribution and incorporate recently updated spatial data where possible. Appendix table 1-1 defines the topology issues referenced in this report.

Data Origination

The BLM provided a national dataset that was housed within the BLM's National Integrated Land System (NILS). However, these data were out-of-date and contained numerous topological errors. Topology is a set of integrity rules that define the behavior of geographically integrated features (Arctur and Zeiler, 2004). We established two topology rules: polygons must not overlap and must not have gaps. Once topology rules were enforced on the 2002 National Data Set, 3,160 errors in the form of slivers, overlapping polygons, and duplications were found covering an area of 5,635 km^2. Many gaps also were identified, but it is not reasonable to tally numbers or area covered because some were not true gaps. These areas were outside of BLM jurisdiction and therefore were likely not considered a gap until adjacent datasets were merged together to form the national dataset. Our analysis sought to differentiate true gaps, such as non-BLM land, reservoirs, canyons, etc., from the false gaps. Overall, errors in topology were largely the result of poor edge matching between state and field office boundaries, although not exclusively.

Methodology

Data Collection

Although a national dataset existed, individual field offices, and in some cases, state offices, maintain and update spatial allotment information on a regular basis. However, many of these data are not integrated into the NILS database, for various reasons. Beginning in late 2007, we contacted BLM State Offices for updated allotment data. At this time, we learned that each State followed a unique protocol regarding the management of allotment data. In some cases, State offices post updated statewide data on their website or State GIS clearinghouse on a regular basis. Other states maintain a fairly regularly updated dataset, but only internally. Alternatively, in some States, field offices are responsible for maintaining their own spatial allotment data, and no state-wide integration is in place. Regardless of the storage location and management level, we contacted appropriate offices to obtain updated data.

Data were collected over the course of 3 years. Spatial data are often dynamic in nature and updates have likely taken place in some offices since we obtained the data. For instance, several field offices provided us with data that were more current than data posted on their website. However, we had to establish a deadline in order to move forward and assemble data into a national dataset. Appendix table 1-2 outlines the dataset and the approximate date that it was collected. Our project area of interest (appendix fig. 1-1) is congruent with the boundary for the conservation assessment of Greater Sage-Grouse and sagebrush habitat conducted by the Western Association of Fish and Wildlife Agencies (Connelly and others, 2004) and is based on the pre-settlement distribution of Greater Sage-Grouse (Schroeder and others, 2004). Therefore, we omitted several field offices from Arizona and New Mexico. The State of Nebraska, assigned to the Newcastle, Wyoming Field Office did not contain any allotments and also was omitted from the analyses.

Initially, we planned to collect spatial data at the pasture level, but decided to focus on the allotment level for two reasons. Spatial data at the pasture level was only readily available at select State and field offices. Second, tabular data on LHS, Billed Use, and most allotment information obtained from field office visits only currently exists at the allotment level.

Assessment of Data

In order to create a national dataset that met our needs, we established a protocol to efficiently create a topologically enforced dataset. The methodology incorporated a series of decision rules and ancillary data such as State and county boundaries, land ownership, 1:24,000 7.5' USGS quadrangles and color-infrared photographs (only used in Wyoming). The protocol intended to minimize subjectivity, but given the scale of the project, some arbitrary decisions were made. The protocol applied to both state level and field office level datasets. Field office datasets from Arizona, Colorado, New Mexico, The Dakotas, and Wyoming were first compiled into State datasets, then loaded into the new, USGS national geodatabase.

An initial assessment of each dataset was undertaken once it was loaded into the geodatabase and subject to topology rules. First, a unique identifier (IDENT in the attribute table) was created by concatenating the two letter state abbreviation with the five digit allotment number. Currently, BLM allotment numbers are unique within a state, therefore the IDENT field created a unique identifier in the national dataset. For example, allotment #00001 in Arizona (IDENT = AZ00001) is differentiated from allotment #00001 in California (IDENT = CA00001) by this attribute. The remaining attributes from the source dataset were converted to match our established scheme. At this time, polygons identified in the attributed table as non-allotments were labeled as "OUT by BLM" to be differentiated from additional out polygons generated by our analysis ("OUT by USGS").

Topology Analysis

Next, topology issues contained within a dataset (that is, spatially internal errors that were not associated with edges of the dataset; appendix fig. 1-2) were identified and corrected using the methodology outlined below. It is important to note that only some state and field office datasets contained topology problems that needed correction. States that maintain more rigorous standards did not have topology issues within the dataset.

Most topology errors were associated with edge matching along State and Field Office boundary lines (appendix fig. 1-2c). Ancillary data such as a shapefiles of state boundaries were obtained from State GIS clearinghouses and BLM State Offices. The boundary dataset with the assumed higher accuracy was used to determine which allotment dataset should be used if there was a conflict. For example, a 1:24,000 boundary dataset would trump a 1:100,000 boundary dataset. If both boundary datasets were developed at the same scale, then 7.5' USGS quadrangles were assessed to identify the most appropriate boundary and which dataset was more accurate. This resulted in a series of decision rules that were used to objectively edge match adjacent State datasets. On occasions where two different allotments occupied the same boundary area and space (for example, Allotment #00001 from State A and Allotment #02050 from State B), the BLM Rangeland Administration System (RAS) database was consulted. If only one of the allotments existed in RAS, then it was retained and the other polygon was deleted. This ensured maximum alignment of potential tabular data when subsequently joining to spatial allotment data. Field office boundaries, or more importantly range allotment management boundaries, are not always congruent with state lines. This was taken into consideration and was occasionally reflected in the adjacent input datasets. For example, the attribute of the polygon in the State A dataset might have indicated that the allotment is actually managed by the adjacent field office in State B. This information was taken into account when it existed.

For small overlaps along edges, we used a majority rule, where for example when two States (or field offices) had an overlapping allotment in their respective datasets, the allotment was merged into the State which contained the majority of the allotment. For gaps along edges of States, the closest allotment on each side of the boundary was extended until meeting at the State boundary line. A similar method was used at the field office level where a State dataset did not exist (Wyoming, Colorado, New Mexico, and Arizona). The State field office boundaries were used to determine edge matching between adjacent field offices.

Land ownership also was used to identify areas that were not or should not be part of the allotment dataset (that is, areas representing true gaps). This was especially difficult along boundaries where one office may have identified it as an 'out' polygon, while the adjacent office displayed it as a gap (no polygon). This situation occurred on BLM lands adjacent to U.S. Department of Defense lands, U.S. Forest Service Lands, Bureau of Indian Affairs Lands, and private lands (in a few instances), but also within allotments where reservoirs, steep canyons, or major streams and road allowances/right of ways may have been excluded (appendix fig. 1-2d).

We attempted to dissolve on the IDENT attribute, which would have represented allotments as either a single or multi-part polygon. (Allotments are not always represented by continuous polygons and may be represented by more than one polygon in the database. For example, one allotment can be separated by landscape features or ownership patterns or represented as a conglomeration of pasture polygons if the input dataset delineated pastures). However, this exercise identified duplicate IDENT attributes within states because input datasets contained duplicate allotment numbers. In many cases the associated polygons likely represent more than one allotment, based on (long) distances between adjacent polygons.

We assumed that polygons with duplicate allotment numbers in close proximity likely belonged to the same (multi-polygon) allotment. We set an arbitrary proximity threshold of three kilometers. If any parts of two or more polygons with the same IDENT were within the three kilometer threshold, then they were considered one allotment. If they fell outside of the threshold, then these polygons were considered duplicate polygon allotments, flagged and moved to a separate feature class. There are likely false positives (actual allotments that have been removed) in this dataset, but we chose to be conservative in establishing the baseline proximity threshold.

Results and Discussion

We developed a final geodatabase that includes three feature classes; Allotments, OUT Polygons, and Duplicate_Polygon_Allotments. The Allotments feature class contains a total of 17,162 allotments. The OUT_polygons feature class contains polygons created by the BLM and the USGS to identify areas within the dataset that do not represent a BLM allotment. These were created to ensure the topology rules were met. The Duplicate_Polygon_Allotments feature class contains 1,806 polygons, which were segregated from the allotment feature class based on our concern that they might represent errors in the dataset (Appendix table 1-3). The vast majority of these are found in the Montana State Office because we had to use the original 2002 National Data for Montana (as we were only able to obtain updated spatial data for one of the field offices administered by the Montana state office, the South Dakota Field Office; Appendix table 1-2). Caution should be used when interpreting our results as false positives likely exist in this dataset, particularly in Montana. Furthermore, the 3 kmbuffer was set to establish baseline proximity, but high variation in distance between adjacent polygons (likely managed as pastures) may exist within some allotments. However, these issues provide an opportunity to address these issues in the future to ensure a high quality national dataset.

This dataset was joined with billed and permitted use data, Land Health Standard data and sagebrush mapping product data for several other analyses referenced in the report. Three file geodatabase tables are included with the spatial dataset. The table "lhs_x_walk" includes the information synthesized by the Land Health Standard analysis (appendix 2). The tables "billed_use" and "permitted_use" were obtained from the BLM RAS database. All three tables can be joined with the allotment feature class on the IDENT attribute.

Users should be aware of the limitations that exist in the dataset. This is a coarse dataset intended for use in a landscape-scale context. The data should not be used as an official allotment demarcation tool. Updates to allotment datasets are made by the BLM at irregular intervals. Therefore this product should be considered a static dataset and treated accordingly. There is not 100 percent agreement between the spatial and tabular datasets. There are some allotments that exist in the spatial data that are not accounted for in the tabular data. Likewise, records exist for allotments in the tabular data that are not present in the spatial data. The partial disagreement between datasets is likely the result of allotment numbers that were changed by BLM, but this assessment provides a potential first step for rectifying these discrepancies to provide a more robust dataset in the future.

References Cited

Arctur, D. and Zeiler, M. 2004. Designing Geodatabases: Case Studies in GIS Data Modeling, ESRI Press.

Connelly, J. W., Knick, S. T. Schroeder, M. A. and Stiver, S. J. 2004. Conservation assessment of greater sage-grouse and sagebrush habitats: Western Association of Fish and Wildlife Agencies, Cheyenne, Wyoming, USA.

Schroeder, M.A., Aldridge, C.L., Apa, A.D., Bohne, J.R., Braun, C.E., Bunnell, S.D., Connelly, J.W., Deibert, P.A., Gardner, S.C., Hilliard, M.A., Kobriger, G.D., McAdam, S.M., McCarthy, C.W., McCarthy, J.J., Mitchell, D.L., Rickerson, E.V. and Stiver, S.J. 2004. Distribution of Sage-Grouse in North America: The Condor, vol, 106, p. 363-376.

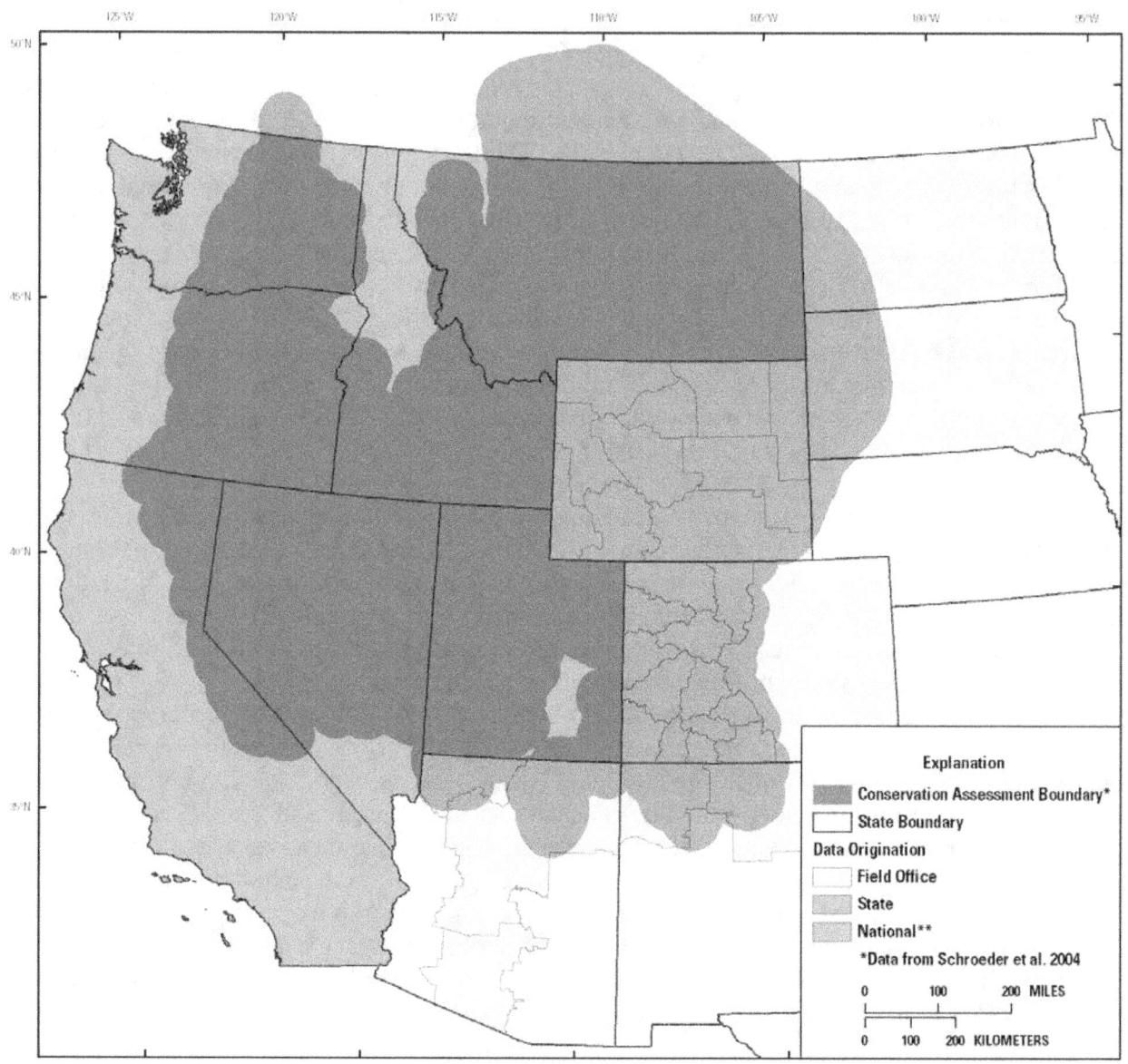

Figure 1-1. Source of original BLM grazing allotment data information used to spatially summarize allotments across area of interest. Area coincides with the conservation assessment of Greater Sage-Grouse and sagebrush habitat conducted by the Western Association of Fish and Wildlife Agencies (Connelly and others, 2004; Schroeder and others, 2004). **Note we were unable to obtain data for the state of Montana so the 2002 National Data Set was used.

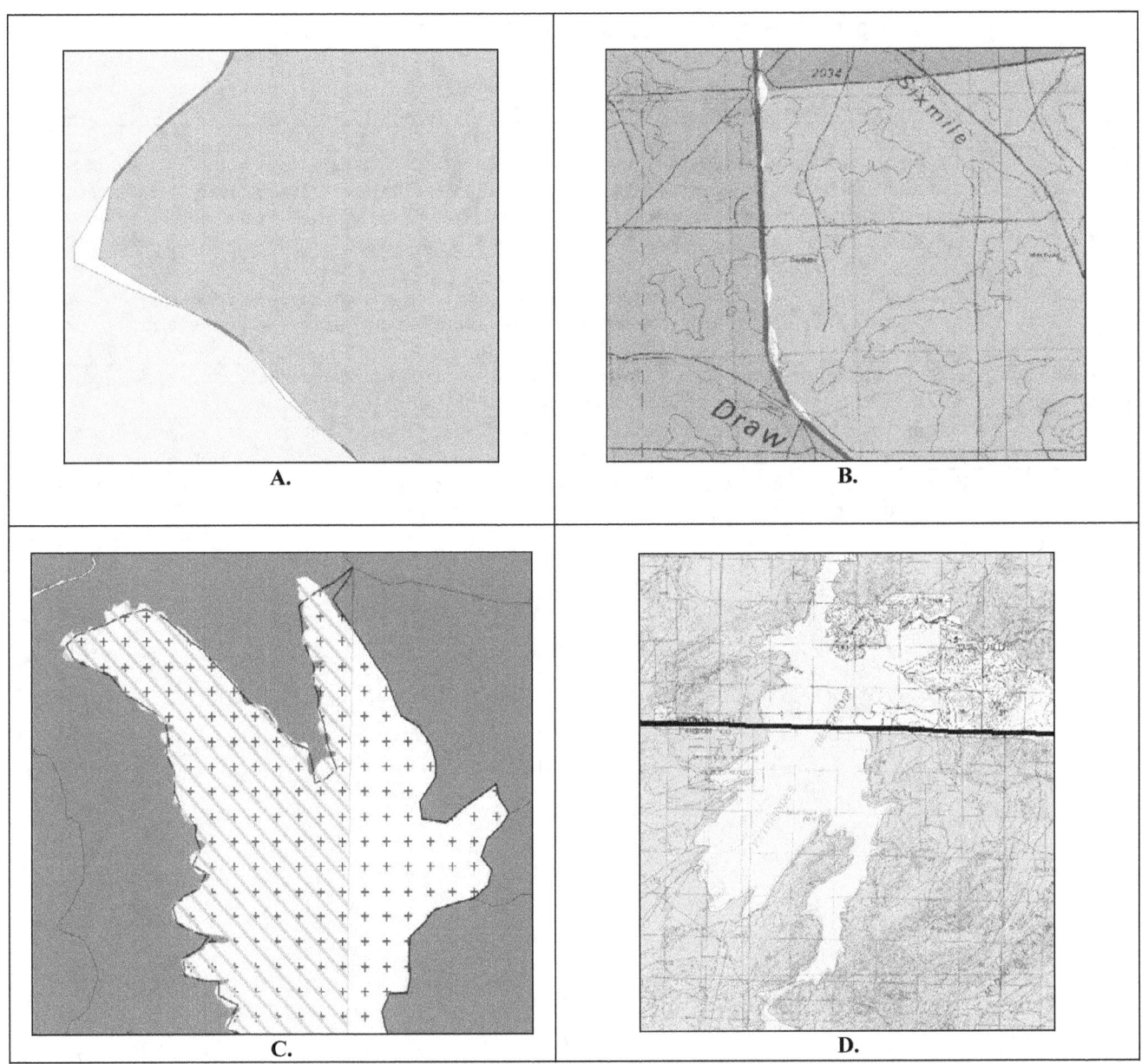

Figure 1-2. Examples of topology and attribute errors associated with edge matching from the BLM national grazing allotment dataset. (a) Sliver polygons (in red) and associated gaps (in white) between two state borders; (b) gaps (in yellow) between allotments bordering a highway; (c) partial duplication (overlap) between adjacent state offices of an allotment (in orange hatch); (d) inconsistency in dataset between field offices where the yellow polygon represents no data and light blue polygon (reservoir) represents a gap that should represent "no data" but is not accounted for in the dataset.

Table 1-1. Definitions of geospatial topology issues that were identified and corrected.

[See appendix figure 1-2 for graphic examples of these common issues]

Issue	Definition
Gap	An empty space between adjacent allotments (appendix fig. 1-2a). False gaps represent a gap in an area where there should not be any space between adjacent allotments. True gaps represent areas where a grazing allotment does not exist (for example, reservoir, highway right of way, land administered by another agency, etc.). "Out polygons" were created for true gaps to ensure that topology could be enforced.
Slivers	A long, narrow polygon can be created during edge matching or some other processing event. These polygons are an artifact of geoprocessing and do not represent any part of an allotment on the ground.
Edge Matching	The edges of source datasets rarely match. These edges represent boundaries between state and/or field offices, and ancillary data must be used to rectify the edge (appendix fig.1-2b).
Duplicate Polygons	In some cases one allotment is represented by two or more polygons that are exact or close in size and shape and located in the same geographic area.
Attributes	Each source dataset has its own set of attributes and codes to describe the data. A consistent attribute scheme was created and employed in the new national dataset.

Table 1-2. Date of spatial allotment data collection from state or field offices across the conservation assessment area for Greater Sage-Grouse.

BLM State Office	Date
California	1/2009
Idaho	8/2008
Montana	2002*
Nevada	4/2008
Oregon	1/2008
Utah	4/2008

*The original national dataset was used for Montana because the state office was unable to provide such data for this project.

State	BLM Field Office	Date
Arizona	Phoenix	7/2008
Arizona	Arizona Strip	12/2007
Colorado	Dolores/Columbine/Pagosa Springs	10/2008
Colorado	Glenwood Springs	10/2008
Colorado	Grand Junction	10/2008
Colorado	Gunnison	10/2008
Colorado	Kremmling	9/2009
Colorado	Little Snake	10/2008
Colorado	Royal Gorge	10/2008
Colorado	Saguache/Del Norte/La Jara	10/2008
Colorado	Uncompaghre	10/2008
Colorado	White River	11/2008
New Mexico	Farmington	3/2009
New Mexico	Taos	3/2009
South Dakota	South Dakota (treated as a MT field office; included North Dakota data)	6/2009
Wyoming	Buffalo	10/2007
Wyoming	Casper	10/2007
Wyoming	Cody	10/2007
Wyoming	Kemmerer	11/2007
Wyoming	Lander	12/2007
Wyoming	Newcastle	11/2007 (from BLM website)
Wyoming	Pinedale	11/2007
Wyoming	Rawlins	10/2007
Wyoming	Rock Springs	7/2008
Wyoming	Worland	12/2007

Table 1-3. Final geodatabase summary of total BLM grazing allotments (# of Allotments) and number of duplicate allotments described for each state within the Greater Sage-Grouse Conservation Assessment area. Duplicates are not included in the allotment count.

State	# of Allotments	# of Duplicates
Arizona	300	4
California	689	0
Colorado	2,429	37
Idaho	2,122	47
Montana (including the Dakotas)	3,761	1,366
New Mexico	541	0
Nevada	750	18
Oregon (including Washington)	1,878	157
Utah	1,275	143
Wyoming	3,417	34
TOTAL	17,162	1,806

Appendix 2. Refinement of BLM Land Health Standards Dataset

Purpose

Our objectives were to (1) examine the status of Land Health Standards (LHS) on Bureau of Land Management (BLM) allotments and (2) in cases of unmet standards, examine whether failure to meet standards was due to livestock.

Data Origination

In 2008, the BLM compiled a dataset which contained results of the most recent LHS evaluations for all BLM allotments; LHS are region-specific (table 2-1), and evaluations are performed by BLM personnel. The original dataset contained the following attributes: administrative state, BLM office code, allotment number, authorization number, date of most recent LHS determination, standards not met and their significant causal factor(s), and authorization status (table 2-2).

We were interested in information at the level of individual grazing allotments. However, raw LHS evaluation data were reported for individual grazing authorizations, and multiple authorizations can be associated with a single allotment.[1] We therefore needed to condense the data to create a one-to-one relationship between allotments and LHS data.

Methodology

We used three decision rules: (1) as long as LHS evaluation data existed for at least one authorization in a given allotment, any other authorizations missing LHS evaluation data were ignored, (2) if there were date discrepancies among authorizations for a given allotment, we conservatively assumed the evaluation was performed on the earliest date, and (3) in some cases where there was conflicting data among authorizations (for whether standards were met on a given allotment). Therefore, if any one of the authorizations indicated a standard was "Not met", the allotment was considered to have "Not met" that standard.

Land Health Standards vary according to region (table 2-1). To make comparisons across states and analyze standards range-wide, we grouped and assigned similar LHS to three main categories of interest: Upland, Riparian, and Biodiversity. In some cases, more than one standard fit into a category (for example, for Colorado, "Native Plant and Animal Communities" and "Threatened and Endangered Species" fell into our Biodiversity category). In those cases, the category was considered "Met" only if all standards were met (for example, in Colorado, *both* "Native Plant and Animal Communities" and "Threatened and Endangered Species" met standards), and was considered "Not met" if at least one standard was not met (e.g., in Colorado, if *either* "Native Plant and Animal Communities" or "Threatened and Endangered Species" did not meet standards)

All allotments were evaluated for these three (Upland, Riparian and Biodiversity) categories, with the exception of eighty allotments (<0.4 percent of all allotments administered by the BLM) in the Mojave area of Nevada that did not have a Riparian standard. The attributes contained in our resulting (standardized) dataset are described in table 2-1.

---

[1] Allotments represent actual spatial delineations on the ground, whereas authorizations reflect the legal grazing description associated with the allotment.

Table 2-1. Bureau of Land Management regional Land Health Standards (LHS), number of allotments in each region, and sources outlining LHS.

[Parentheses indicate which LHS standards were placed into Upland (U), Riparian (R), or Biodiversity (B) categories. We did not include water quality, air quality, seedings, exotic plant communities, ecosystem components, wild horse/burro, or cultural resources in our categorization or analyses]

BLM LHS Regions	LHS Standards	Number of Allotments	Source
Arizona	Uplands (U) Riparian (R) Biodiversity – native species, special status species, desired species (B)	795	http://rangelandswest.arid.arizona.edu/rangelandswest/jsp/hottopics/legal/policy/azstandards/azstandardsstandards.jsp
Northwestern California and Central California Regions	Soils (U) Species (B) Riparian (R) Water Quality	331	http://www.blm.gov/ca/st/en/prog/grazing.html
Northeastern California and Northwestern Nevada Regions	Upland Soils (U) Streams (R) Water Quality Riparian and Wetland Sites (R) Biodiversity (B)	116	http://www.blm.gov/ca/st/en/prog/grazing.html
California Desert Region	Upland Soils (U) Riparian and Wetland (R) Stream Channel Morphology (R) Native Species (B)	51	Appendix 4: Fundamentals of Rangeland Health and Standards and Guidelines for Grazing Administration (43 CFR 4180), Section 4180.2 (f)
Colorado	Upland Soils (U) Riparian Systems (R) Native Plant and Animal Communities (B) Threatened and Endangered Species (B) Water Quality	2088	http://www.blm.gov/co/st/en/BLM_Programs/grazing/rm_stds_guidelines.html
Idaho Idaho cont.	Watersheds (U) Riparian and Wetlands (R) Stream Channel/Floodplain (R) Native Plant Communities (B) Seedings Exotic Plant Communities Water Quality Threatened and Endangered Plant and Animal Species (B)	1945	http://www.blm.gov/pgdata/etc/medialib/blm/id/publications.Par.91993.File.dat/SGFinal.pdf
Montana (including North Dakota and South Dakota)	Uplands (U) Riparian and Wetlands (R) Water Quality Air Quality Native Plant and Animal Habitat or Biodiversity (B)	5000	http://www.blm.gov/mt/st/en/prog/grazing.1.html

64

Table 2-1. Bureau of Land Management regional Land Health Standards (LHS), number of allotments in each region, and sources outlining LHS.—Continued

[Parentheses indicate which LHS standards were placed into Upland (U), Riparian (R), or Biodiversity (B) categories. We did not include water quality, air quality, seedings, exotic plant communities, ecosystem components, wild horse/burro, or cultural resources in our categorization or analyses]

Region	Standards	Number of allotments	Source
New Mexico	Upland Sites (U) Biotic Communities including Threatened and Endangered Species (B) Riparian Sites (R)	2152	http://www.blm.gov/pgdata/etc/medialib/blm/nm/field_offices/nmso/nmso_planning/nmso_misc_planning.Par.47309.File.dat/memo-RMPA.pdf
Nevada – Mojave and Southern Great Basin	Soils (U) Ecosystem Components Habitat/Biota (B) Wild Horse/Burros	80	http://www.blm.gov/nv/st/en/prog/grazing/grazing_s_gs.html
Nevada – Sierra Front and Northwestern Nevada	Soils (U) Riparian/Wetlands (R) Water Quality Plant /Animal Habitat (B) Special Status/Threatened and Endangered Species (B)	184	http://www.blm.gov/nv/st/en/prog/grazing/grazing_s_gs.html
Nevada – Northeastern Great Basin	Uplands (U) Riparian/Wetlands (R) Habitat (B) Cultural Resources Healthy Wild Horse/Burros	482	http://www.blm.gov/nv/st/en/prog/grazing/grazing_s_gs.html
Oregon	Uplands (U) Riparian (R) Ecological Processes (B) Water Quality Habitat for Threatened and Endangered Species (B)	1810	http://www.blm.gov/or/resources/recreation/csnm/files/rangeland_standards.pdf
Utah Utah cont.	Upland Soils (U) Riparian/Wetlands (R) Desired Species (natives, threatened and endangered, special status) (B) Water Quality	1380	http://www.blm.gov/ut/st/en/fo/vernal/grazing_/rangeland_health_standards.html
Wyoming	Soils (U) Riparian/Wetlands (R) Upland Vegetation (U) Habitat for Threatened and Endangered Species (B) Water Quality Air Quality	3433	http://www.blm.gov/wy/st/en/programs/grazing/standards_and_guidelines/standards.html

Table 2-2. Attribute table of original Bureau of Land Management Land Health Standards (LHS) dataset and description of attributes

Attribute	Description
Administrative State	BLM State Office under which allotment jurisdiction falls
Office Code	BLM field office under which allotment jurisdiction falls
Allotment Number	unique identification number associated with allotment
Authorization Number	unique identification number for grazing permits associated with allotments
Date of most recent Land Health Determination	date of most recent evaluation of whether allotment is meeting state LHS
Land Health Standard(s) not achieved in the Allotment and significant causal factor(s) identified	indicates which, if any, LHS not achieved and identifies causal factor
Authorization Status	indicates grazing permits put on a "hold" status (i.e. grazing no longer authorized)

Table 2-3. Attributes associated with final standardized Land Health Standards (LHS) dataset .

Attribute(s)	Description	Values
Administrative State	BLM State Office under which allotment jurisdiction falls	State Abbreviation (e.g. **AZ**, **CO**, **WY**, etc.)
Office Code	BLM field office under which allotment jurisdiction falls	BLM Administrative Office Code
Allotment Number	unique identification number associated with allotment	Numerical
Authorization Number	unique identification number for grazing permits associated with allotments	Numerical
Year LHS Performed	Year most recent LHS determination performed (according to USGS assumptions)	Year (e.g., **2002**) **9999** = not completed **8888** = allotment exempted from LHS requirements **7777** = no information given
U, R, B	Indicates whether following standards were met: U = Upland, Upland Soils, Soils, Upland Vegetation, Watersheds LHS R = Riparian, wetlands, streams, stream channel LHS B = Biodiversity, Biotic Communities, Native Species, Native and Desired Plant Communities and Habitat, Ecological Processes, and Special Status Species Standards	**N** = No **Y** = Yes **NA** = Not Applicable **NC** = Evaluation Not Completed
U_L, R_L, B_L	Indicates whether failure to meet a standard was due to livestock grazing	**N** = No **Y** = Yes **NA** = Not Applicable **NC** = Evaluation Not Completed **NI** = Not Indicated
All_Stds_URB_LS	Indicates if one or more of the Upland, Riparian or Biodiversity standards were unmet due to livestock	**PASS** = if all standards met or not applicable **LS** = if livestock caused at least one standard to be unmet **No_LS** = if any standards were unmet and none due to livestock **NC** = if all standards were not completed
Pct_Fail_URB_LS	Ratio of number of standards not met to number of standards	Numerical NC = LHS not completed

Table 2-3. Attributes associated with final standardized Land Health Standards (LHS) dataset .—Continued

NumStdsFailing_URB_LS	Number of standards that indicate livestock as a causal factor for failure to meet standards	Numerical
Num_Stds_URB	Number of U, R, B, standards present (i.e. a count of 3 means all are present)	Numerical **9999** = LHS not completed
All_Stds_LS	If one or more regional allotment standards were unmet due to livestock	**PASS** = if all standards were met or not applicable **LS** = if livestock caused at least one standard to be unmet **No_LS** = if any standards were unmet and none due to livestock **NC** = if all standards were not completed
Pct_Fail_LS	Ratio of number of unmet regional allotment standards to total number of regional standards	Numerical (ratio) **NC** = LHS not completed
NumStdsFailing_LS	Number of regional standards that indicate livestock as a causal factor for not meeting standard	Numerical (**count data**)
Num_Stds	Number of regional standards for evaluation	Numerical (count data) 9999 = LHS not completed

Appendix 3. ESD Sites and Selection Protocol

We sought to field-validate estimates of potential vegetation production reported in the Natural Resources Conservation Service (NRCS) Ecological Site Information System (ESIS). Ecological Site Descriptions (ESDs) contained in ESIS report rangeland site information such as plant community types and site characteristics (for example, elevation, climate). Because ESDs are linked to soil map units, we first inspected soil survey data coverage across Bureau of Land Management (BLM) land. We in turn selected BLM land located in Harney County, Oregon, as our area of focus because it was an area within our study region with full coverage in the NRCS Soil Survey Geographic Database (SSURGO). We then identified soil map units within this area associated with a single ESD (as opposed to multiple ecological sites scattered throughout a map unit). Because growth curve information was required for our method of assessing production (see below), we eliminated ecological sites that did not contain growth curves in their ESDs. From the resulting dataset, we chose nine common ecological sites (table 3-1) where we would compare our own field production estimates to the estimates found in the site-specific Ecological Site Descriptions.

In June 2010, we made estimates of production at forty-two randomly located points across the nine ecological sites (table 3-1) after verifying soil types and ecological sites. All occurred within the Central Rocky and Blue Mountain Foothill Major Land Resource Area (OR-MLRA 010). For ease of sampling, points were located 75–200 m from improved roads and where slope was <50. Points within an ecological site type were >250 m apart (fig. 1). Points were located >200 m from water features that were likely to have concentrated livestock activity in their immediate vicinities (perennial streams and water bodies, and Burns BLM District GIS point features identified as DAM, DIKE, DRAIN, DUGOUT, GUZZLER, POND, RESERVOIR, SILT BASIN, SPIGOT, SPRING, TANK, TROUGH, VALVE, VALVE/VENT, VENT, WATERHOLE, WELL).

We used the NRCS Reconstruction Method (U.S. Department of Agriculture, Natural Resources Conservation Service, 2006), which entails making visual estimates of production-by-weight for individual plant species and correcting for variables such as herbivory, time of year, and rainfall. At each of the forty-two points we sampled along two 50 m transects, oriented north and east. We placed a 1×1 m quadrat every 10 meters (between 10 and 50 m) along each transect where we made production estimates of all herbaceous species. We then compared those on-the-ground production estimates of herbaceous cover to estimates for those sites contained in the ESIS database (fig. 2).

References Cited

U.S. Department of Agriculture, Natural Resources Conservation Service, 2006, Chapter 4: Inventorying and monitoring grazing land resources, National range and pasture handbook.

Table 3-1. NRCS Ecological Sites sampled.

N=	NRCS Site	Name and Precipitation	Elevation (m)
9	R010XB080OR	JD MOUNTAIN CLAYPAN 12-16 PZ	3,000-5,700
7	R010XC032OR	SR MOUNTAIN CLAYEY 12-16 PZ	4,800-6,000
4	R010XB028OR	JD SHRUBBY MOUNTAIN CLAYEY 12-16 PZ	4,000-6,000
4	R010XC080OR	SR MAHOGANY MOUNTAIN LOAM 14-18 PZ	4,000-7,500
4	R010XC047OR	SR MOUNTAIN SOUTH 12-16 PZ	3,500-6,000
4	R010XC066OR	SR MOUNTAIN NORTH 12-16 PZ	4,500-6,000
6	R010XC021OR	SR CLAYEY 9-12 PZ	2,000-3,500
2	R010XC030OR	SR MOUNTAIN LOAMY 9-12 PZ	3,500-4,200
2	R010XC065OR	SR MOUNTAIN NORTH 9-12 PZ	3,200-4,500

Appendix 4. Fundamentals of Rangeland Health Outlined in 43 CFR 4180.1

1. (a) Watersheds are in, or are making significant progress toward, properly functioning physical condition, including their upland, riparian-wetland, and aquatic components; soil and plant conditions support infiltration, soil moisture storage, and the release of water that are in balance with climate and landform and maintain or improve water quality, water quantity, and timing and duration of flow.

2. (b) Ecological processes, including the hydrologic cycle, nutrient cycle, and energy flow, are maintained, or there is significant progress toward their attainment, in order to support healthy biotic populations and communities.

3. (c) Water quality complies with State water quality standards and achieves, or is making significant progress toward achieving, established BLM management objectives such as meeting wildlife needs.

4. (d) Habitats are, or are making significant progress toward being, restored or maintained for Federal threatened and endangered species, Federal proposed or candidate threatened and endangered species, and other special status species.